The Hammer

THE BEST OF HANK AARON
FROM THE PAGES OF SPORTS ILLUSTRATED

EDITED BY
CHRISTIAN STONE AND
MARK MRAVIC

SPORTS ILLUSTRATED BOOKS

CONTENTS

EDITOR'S NOTE: The stories in this collection are a reflection of their time as well as of their subject matter, Henry Aaron. Usages that seem anachronistic or inappropriate, such as the word "Negro," have been preserved, to better convey the historical and cultural context in which the original stories appeared.

$\Diamond$

Introduction

THE HOME RUN KING NEVER DID DO MAJESTY WELL. HIS home runs left the park in a hurry and with an economy of scale, rarely bothering to travel much farther or higher than needed. He could do everything on a baseball field with ease, but because his game and his words lacked unnecessary ornamentation, he never invited undo attention to himself.

They called Henry Louis Aaron Hammerin' Hank, an encomium to his bluntly effective hitting but one that works just as well as a tribute to his entire ethos. Hammering is the life's work of commoners rather than of kings. It is generally not a pursuit to which heroic movies, elegiac poems or, apparently, magazine covers are dedicated. (Aaron appeared on just three SPORTS ILLUSTRATED covers in his 23-year career). In hammering, as in Aaron, however, there is an understated nobility that only the passage of time adequately reveals.

For instance, not one of Aaron's single-season home run totals is listed among the 68 highest of all time, but he pounded out 755 homers in his career, more than any player before him—and without suspicion of chemical enhancement. None of his single-season RBI totals rank among the top 100, but he is the alltime career leader in that category as well. What he did was build the Egyptian pyramids of a baseball career, the finished product a monument as much to man's persistence as to his reach.

Aaron was such a masterly hitter that he would have passed

3,000 hits even if he never hit a home run in his life. He won three Gold Gloves, received MVP votes 19 straight years, and stole bases at a 76% success rate. He famously outhomered the Babe. He did as much for the racial integration of the sport as any man who followed Jackie Robinson. And yet somehow Aaron, in the pantheon of baseball gods and in the fabric of American culture, is an underrated and underappreciated presence. It must have been the monotony of all that hammering.

This book is a tribute to Hammerin' Hank, an appreciation of the man and his life's work both on the field and off. The number 755 always will be his, no matter what follows, as much as 56 is the perpetual property of Joe DiMaggio and 61 of Roger Maris. It is what made him king, in a statistical sense, anyway.

"The most basic motivation," Aaron wrote in his 1991 autobiography, *I Had a Hammer*, about surpassing Ruth's 714 home runs, "was the pure ambition to break such an important and longstanding barrier. Along with that would come the recognition that I thought was long overdue me."

But 755 is, even by his own estimation, an incomplete measure of the ballplayer and the man. Aaron wrote that he regarded his total bases record as more representative of "what I was all about as a hitter. . . . It also tells me something that the record had been [Stan] Musial's, because I consider myself to be much more like Musial than Ruth, both as a hitter and as a person."

This book connects the dots of Aaron's baseball life, from a 1957 SI piece that falls harshly on the ears—given the sensibilities of today—about a "rather indolent-looking young man," to a '73 article about "A Torturous Road to 715," to a moving 1992 piece about his painful memories of traveling that road. It is an unflinching reminder of what Aaron endured as much as of what he accomplished.

As a teenager in 1953, Aaron, along with teammates Felix Mantilla and Horace Garner, integrated the Sally League in the Deep South, putting up with taunts and threats from fans and living in separate quarters from his white teammates—all while hitting .362 and being named league MVP. Two decades later, as he chased and ultimately passed Ruth, he received thousands of racially charged hate letters. Atlanta, his adoptive home city, gave him little support. On the night he hit his 711th homer, for instance, there were only 1,362 people in Atlanta Stadium. Many who did come to the ballpark in those years heckled him. Wrote Aaron, "At the very least, I felt I had earned the right not to be verbally abused and racially ravaged in my home ballpark." There was fear that it might have been worse.

In September 1998, Aaron watched wistfully as Mark McGwire crossed home plate following his record-breaking 62nd home run and hugged his son, Matthew, dressed in full Cardinals uniform as a team batboy. When Aaron hit 715, his daughter, Gaile, had to watch on television while under the protection of FBI agents, due to threats upon his family.

Despite the hatred, Aaron played with a cool dignity. "Grace in a gray flannel suit," as the great Jim Murray observed. But Aaron also spoke out against injustice when he saw it, whether as a player, baseball executive or businessman. In this world, Longfellow wrote, a man must be either anvil or hammer. Hank Aaron left no doubt about which he was.   —*Tom Verducci*

◇

THE RISING

◇

Murder with a
Blunt Instrument

BY ROY TERRELL

Only 23, "Mr. Wrists" was already being called the
league's best righthanded hitter since Rogers Hornsby

THE MILWAUKEE BRAVES ARE STICKING RIGHT IN THE
middle of a riotous pennant race, in spite of multiple injuries
and a subpar performance from their famed pitching staff.
The man who has supplied most of the glue is Henry Louis
Aaron, and if his contributions fail to do the job once again
this year, perhaps the only hope remaining for Milwaukee
would be to get Ty Cobb on waivers from the American
League. Certainly no one else could do any more.

Aaron is the rather indolent-looking young man who showed
up on the first day of spring training at Bradenton, Fla., in 1956,
sauntered casually to the plate in the gray road uniform of the
Braves, swished a borrowed bat back and forth a couple of
times, and then hit the first three pitches out of the park.

"Ol' Hank," he pronounced, "is ready."

No one fell over in surprise. Ol' Hank, who wasn't really so
old (having just turned 22 at the time), was always supposed

to hit the baseball and almost always seems to have been ready. From the day he first reported to the Braves in the spring of 1954, a scared 20-year-old with less than two seasons of experience in the lower minors behind him, the entire Milwaukee organization had been acting strangely like a family that had discovered a uranium mine in its backyard. That first season Aaron hit .280 and was second only to Wally Moon of the Cardinals in the voting for Rookie of the Year. The next year he hit .314 and drove in 106 runs. Now—Ol' Hank having had time to look around a bit and get the feel of the big leagues—things were expected to pop.

That they haven't popped, at least not enough to bring Milwaukee its first pennant, is assuredly not the fault of Hank Aaron. In 1956, proving that he was indeed ready, he hit .328 to win the National League batting championship and became the only player in baseball to reach 200 hits. As the Braves blew past the St. Louis Cardinals into first place in early August (for keeps, it would turn out), Hank was slashing his way toward the first Triple Crown since Joe Medwick accomplished the feat some 20 years before. What would have been considered heresy a year ago, people were now prepared to accept as simple fact: This slender, 23-year-old Negro from Mobile, Alabama is the best righthand hitter seen in the National League since the days of Rogers Hornsby.

Perhaps the most unusual part of the Aaron story is the fact that no one gets very excited about it. Sometimes it is even easy to forget that Henry Aaron is around. Without the physical proportions or explosive speed of a Mickey Mantle, without the breathtaking color of a Willie Mays, without the long and brilliant—and controversial—career of a Ted Williams, Aaron seems to be hardly a personality at all. He says practically nothing, stays out of nightclubs, never loses his cap running the bases, and spits only upon the ground. He has not even had time to become the quiet but lethal legend which is Musial. All he does is walk up to the plate four or five times a day to hit a baseball.

It is then, however, during those brief moments, that the thousands wake up and realize, almost too late, that here before them stands one of the divinely gifted few. He looks small down there in the batter's box and not very deadly at all. He stands well away from the plate, toward the rear of the box, languidly swinging the yellowish-white bat in a low arc. Then the pitcher stretches and throws, Aaron cocks his bat and the ball comes in. At the last moment he strides forward and leans toward the baseball; the bat comes whipping around in a blur almost too fast for the eye to follow and there is a sharp, loud report. A white streak flashes through the infield or into the outfield or over the fence, and Henry Aaron has another base hit. Sometimes he does this two or three times a day. Some days, because he is human, he doesn't do it at all. But, occasionally, because he is Hank Aaron, he does it four or five times. It is this which sets him apart.

One day Birdie Tebbetts was moaning about how Johnny Logan and Del Crandall of the Braves always murdered his Reds. "How about Aaron?" someone asked. "Aaron," said Birdie, "murders *everybody*."

Just why is Aaron murdering everybody? One explanation is the wrists, of course. Everyone knows about them. "Best wrists in baseball," says Fred Haney. "Best wrists in baseball," says Tebbetts. "Best wrists in baseball," says the man in shirtsleeves up in Section 27, Row 13, Seat 5 to his friend in Seat 6, who only glares because he was going to say it himself as soon as he swallowed the rest of his hot dog.

The wrists are good. They are almost eight inches around and the forearms ripple with little knots of muscle whenever Henry curls his big, oversized hands around the handle of a bat. And despite the trim, 31-inch waist, it takes a size 42 uniform shirt to cover the sloping, powerful shoulders and muscular back and chest.

"He's like a rock," says Doc Feron, the Braves' trainer. "Smooth muscled but hard. And, you know, he's not really so little, either. He just looks like it in his uniform. Henry's a pretty big boy."

Anywhere but on an athletic field filled with 200-pounders, Aaron would be considered a pretty big boy. He is 5' 11½" tall and weighs 178 pounds. But there is more to it than wrists and forearms and muscles and size. He also has exceptional eyesight and a natural rhythm and sense of timing unsurpassed in all baseball. "It's fantastic," says Braves ace Warren Spahn, "how long he can look at a pitch before he decides whether to swing. It's as good as giving him an extra strike." But perhaps most important of all, Aaron is a fine hitter because of one fundamental belief: A baseball is made to be hit.

At the moment of impact in Henry's swing, the weight is far

forward on the front foot, more so than any other player in the game today. It is a position reached by intent rather than chance. An offensive hitter, as opposed to many ballplayers who are concerned only with protecting the plate or themselves, Aaron is always going out to meet the ball, to attack it. He considers the bunt a fine tactic so long as it is employed by someone else; a base on balls is absolutely no fun at all.

There are those who believe Aaron might hit .400 if he would take a few walks when he finds them, lay down a bunt now and then and lay off the bad pitches. He is a notorious bad ball hitter whose strike zone was once described by ex-Braves manager Charlie Grimm as "a general area ranging from the top of his head to his toes." And when Aaron was playing in the Class A Sally League an opposing pitcher once warned a teammate not to waste time dusting him off. "The last two I threw at his head," the pitcher said, "he hit out of the park."

But no one is absolutely convinced that he won't someday hit .400 anyway.

BORN IN Mobile on Feb. 5, 1934, Henry grew up with his five brothers and three sisters in one of the better-class Negro residential sections, called Toulminville. He was a quiet boy who liked sports—basketball, softball—and books. This may come as a slight shock to some members of the National League, who swear they never saw Henry—even in those rare moments when he remained awake long enough to read—get any closer to the public library than the comic book rack at the corner newsstand. But his mother says it is true and that he was a good student. Besides, there are a lot of things the National League hasn't figured out yet about Henry Aaron.

He played baseball one summer in the city recreation league and must have been a pretty impressive rookie even then; upon graduation from Central High in 1952 Aaron signed a contract with the Indianapolis Clowns, a touring Negro professional team, and set out by bus to see the world. He got only far enough for organized baseball, in the person of a Braves scout named Dewey Griggs, to see him and like him.

The Braves bought him for $10,000 on a 30-day look and sent him to Eau Claire, Wis., in the Class C Northern League to play shortstop. By the time he had been there two days, manager Bill Adair had seen far too much to send him back. After Henry had been there a week, he was named to the league All-Star team. He finished the season hitting .336 and was named rookie of the year.

At Jacksonville the next year, Aaron led the Sally League in everything but peanut sales: batting (.362), runs batted in (125), hits, runs, doubles and most hours slept for day, week and season.

"The most relaxed kid I ever saw," says Ben Geraghty, who now manages the Braves Triple-A farm club at Wichita but who was at Jacksonville that year. "From the time he got on the bus until we got to the next town, Hank was asleep. Nothing ever bothered him."

Henry also led the league in most errors for a second baseman, and it was then that the Braves decided he would become an outfielder. But no one ever attempted to alter his batting style. Paul Waner, the famed Milwaukee hitting coach, soon sent word up through the organization that everyone was to keep their hands off when Aaron walked to the plate. "He's got a perfect swing now," warned Waner. "Don't anyone try to change him. Just let him alone."

"The most natural hitter I ever saw," says Geraghty. "He would go out to hit—you couldn't keep him out of the batting cage—and he didn't seem to make any difference.

"He hit a home run off Gene Conley one day when we were playing Toledo in an exhibition game. 'What bat did you use, Henry?' the next hitter asked him. 'The Greenberg model,' Henry said. 'You couldn't,' the other fellow told him. 'I've got the Greenberg model.' 'Well,' Henry said, 'anyway, I was usin' a bat. It must have been the right one.'

"He hasn't really changed, I guess. This year in spring training, after he won the batting championship, I asked him what kind of bat he was using now. Figured he'd say 'a Babe Ruth handle with a Hornsby barrel' or something like that. He said 'I've got me two bats now. A long one and a short one. I use the long one when they're pitchin' me outside and the short one when they're pitchin' me inside.' "

It is fairly easy to find oneself completely beguiled by the soporific, almost indifferent exterior which cloaks Henry's rather highly developed sense of humor. He had everyone at Jacksonville convinced that he didn't know the names of the opposing players, of the opposing team, of the town he was in or, frequently, of even his own teammates. He once told a writer he had developed his wrists by delivering ice when he was a kid; the only job he really ever had in those days was helping a man care for people's lawns. Breaking out of a slump, he told teammates that in desperation he had called Stan Musial for advice and that Stan told him to "keep swinging, boy, just keep swinging." Later, Musial had to laugh. "The only time I ever saw Henry up until then," he said, "all I said was 'hello.' " He also told an interviewer his favorite pastime was hunting. Another, who knew him better and knew that Henry liked to listen to modern music and go to the movies but was unaware he had ever shot anything bigger than a game of pool, saw the story. "I didn't know you hunted, Henry," he said. "I don't," said Aaron. "It's too dangerous."

The best proof that Aaron was a pretty intelligent young man even at the age of 19 is the fact that he was smart enough that year at Jacksonville to stay relaxed. Along with Felix Mantilla, now a teammate with the Braves, and an outfielder named Horace Garner, he was the first Negro to play in the Deep South Sally League. He had to live with a Negro family in town and, on the road, room in Negro hotels. Frequently he had to remain on the bus while white teammates brought his meals out to him from roadside restaurants. And at season's end, having said almost nothing and done quite a lot, there were no complaints about Henry Aaron by either the ballplayers in the league or the fans who watched him play.

Even now Aaron makes no attempt to convince anyone that he is a mental giant. When asked why he liked the outfield better than the infield, Henry told a reporter: "There's less to do out there. Especially thinking."

He is generally regarded, however, as an above-average

defensive ballplayer who could be even better if he wanted to badly enough. Even the Braves admit that he has a tendency to get a little lazy. But he has a good, strong arm—although not an exceptional one—and very good hands; he catches everything he gets to and gets to most baseballs that he should with a long, loping stride that covers more ground than it would appear. Once the Braves tried to get him up on his toes, to dig hard when he ran, but when his batting average began to tail off, they abandoned the project like a hot coal. When you ask Henry now why he doesn't run harder, he grins a little and says: "I'm pacin' myself."

THE BRAVES tell the story of the day in Aaron's rookie year when the youngster hit a home run off Robin Roberts. "Man," he said later, "was that really Mr. Roberts?" At the time, everyone believed him. Now the Braves will tell you he probably knew not only who Roberts was but what he had for breakfast and what size sweatshirt he wore.

In one respect, however, all pitchers are alike to Henry. "When my timin' is on," he says, "it don't make any difference who the pitcher is. I hit anybody then. When it's off, I don't."

Usually the timing is on and he has a great deal of quiet confidence that it is the pitcher who should be doing the worrying. "I've got a bat," he says, "and all the pitcher's got is a ball. I figure that gives me the edge."

Because he has never considered himself to be a particularly powerful hitter, Aaron has wisely refused to get involved in the home run craze. He simply tries to meet the ball, wherever it is pitched, and let those wrists take care of the rest. He hit only 27 home runs in 1955 and 26 in '56 and insists that he wasn't trying to hit home runs in '57.

"Whatever I'm doin'," he says, "I don't want to know what it is. I just want to keep on doin' it."

He does know that he is hitting the ball up in the air more this year and, trying to be helpful, once suggested it might be because he was standing up straighter at the plate. The real reasons are probably even simpler: he began the '57 season using a 34-ounce bat instead of his usual 36-ounce one and can whip it around even faster; he weighs almost 10 pounds more than when he first came up to the big leagues, and he knows more about the pitchers—and about hitting—than he did one or two years ago.

AARON STILL sends the ball ripping to all fields, and almost as many of his home runs have disappeared over the rightfield fences this season as have been pulled to left. Because of this, no defense has been able to shift on him. And certainly no pitcher has yet found his weakness. When the Giants stopped him with only two singles in three games at the start of the season, Bill Rigney triumphantly announced: "I think we've found a way to pitch to Aaron." In his next 27 at bats against the Giants, Hank had 12 hits.

Outside of opposing pitchers, who may be excused, Aaron hasn't an enemy in the world. He gives Haney and the Milwaukee coaches no trouble, acts "like a big leaguer," according to Joe Taylor, the Braves equipment man and clubhouse manager, and is held in high regard both professionally and personally by his teammates, who rib him unmercifully, then praise him to the skies when his back is turned. Even the umpires love him. If a pitch is close enough to be questionable, Henry is going to hit it—or at least try to. "I don't give those umpires any call," says Henry, "to have words with me."

The Braves say Aaron is so relaxed at the plate that he catches catnaps between pitches. They know, however, that this is deceptive: One day an accomplished veteran, while watching Aaron in the batter's box, was startled at the careless way Henry was holding the bat. "You better turn the trademark up," he rashly suggested.

"Yogi," Aaron told Yogi Berra with a withering look, "I didn't come up here to read."

◇

POSTSCRIPT: *Aaron would finish the '57 season with a NL-leading 44 home runs and 132 RBIs, but fell short of the batting (and Triple) crown by 29 points. There were, however, larger rewards to be reaped. On Sept. 23 Aaron would clinch the pennant for the Braves, the city's first, with a walkoff home run against the Cardinals. He would hit .393 with three homers against the Yankees in the World Series, which Milwaukee won in seven games. The following month, he won the NL MVP—remarkably the only one he received in his 23-year career.*

◇

Danger with A Double A

BY JACK MANN

*Neither age nor the Braves' move down South changed
Bad Henry one bit. He just keeps swinging—and connecting*

"I'M THIS MANY," SAID DORINDA AARON, HOLDING UP four fingers, "and I'm going to have a party." She will be five years old next Feb. 5, a day when National League pitchers might well raise a cup of cheer, because Dorinda's daddy, Bad Henry, will be 33. Their enemy grows older.

But not so much that you could notice. "I can serve you a beer," the lady in the sweltering Atlanta airport said to Aaron's companion, "but this young man will have to show me his I.D. card."

"Why, that man is 30 years old," the other lady said.

"Damn," Henry said, flabbergasted and delighted. "Damn. I thought she was putting me on."

"That's what I told you, Henry," said Atlanta Braves president John McHale. "Don't ever get older than 30."

The greatest cross-handed hitter in the history of the Negro American League has ballooned to 180 pounds in the 14 years since the Braves gave him a ticket to Eau Claire, and orders to keep his right hand on top, but the extra 10 pounds are packed neatly around his chest cavity. In the body of a sophomore halfback Henry Aaron has developed the mind of a computer, and he'll be the next 3,000-hit man unless Willie Mays beats him to it. Or unless he suffers a crippling injury. Don't count on the latter. Aaron has averaged 153 games a season since he broke an ankle in 1954, his rookie year.

"He not only knows what the pitch will be," says Ron Perranoski, the Dodgers relief pitcher who has held Bad Henry to an .812 average (13 for 16) in six seasons, "but where it will be. He's hit one home run off me [out of centerfield in Dodger Stadium], and he went after that pitch as if he'd called for it."

"It was a fast ball, high and away," said Aaron, who can recite the locus and characteristics of each of the 26 pitches he hit for home runs in the first half of the season. "It was the first pitch, and I guess I was looking for it. I figured he'd try to set me up for the sinker."

"Pitchers don't set Henry up," said teammate Gene Oliver. "He sets them up. I honestly believe he intentionally looks bad on a certain pitch just so he'll get it again."

"Well, not too often," Aaron said. "But say it's a breaking pitch that's going to hit on the plate. I might let my tail fly out a little and miss it and look foolish. Then the pitcher might throw that same pitch for a strike some other time—with two on."

This may be Aaron's first 50-homer season, and it might not be the last. When he arrived at the All-Star break with his 26 homers and a batting average near his career low of .280, it was logical to assume he had altered his formula, determined to pull the ball toward instant money. Henry is making more than $75,000, proving that guys who hit .320 lifetime can ride in Buick Rivieras, but he can read and sees six-digit numbers on the sports pages.

"That doesn't bother me," Henry said. "If I'd played in New York, I'd have made a lot more money. There were only those two papers in Milwaukee, and that makes a difference. Anyway, these people have been good to me, and you don't miss what you don't have."

And you like what you have if you rode the bus with the Indianapolis Clowns in the Negro league, playing a double-header in Washington and a single in Baltimore the same day, then climbing back on the bus to try to sleep on the way to Buffalo. (By the time Milwaukee scout Dewey Griggs offered Aaron $50 a month more than the Giants did, he was leading the Negro AL with a .467 average, having been converted from cross-handed hitting by Clown owner Syd Pollock. "Not completely," Henry says. "If I got two strikes on me and my back was to the dugout so they couldn't see me, I'd sneak the left hand up on top.")

But why so many home runs this year, and most of them to leftfield? The stance and the swing haven't changed. "No," Aaron said, "but I don't go up there swinging at what they throw me anymore. I've studied and concentrated, and now I wait until I get my pitch."

"He sure as hell does," said Sandy Koufax. "Did you see him go after that curve I hung for him today? That was a mistake, and you don't get away with a mistake to Bad Henry. He's the last guy I want to see coming up there."

There was talk that Roberto Clemente once held that distinction. "That was two years ago," Koufax said. "Some guys give me more trouble one year than another. But Aaron is always the same. He's just Bad Henry."

"This game looks easy," says Bad Henry, "but it's—well— not a guessing game, but a thinking game. Too many people think it's simple."

TOO MANY people think Aaron is simple, and relaxed, and insouciant—a nerveless bundle of sinew with mongoose reflexes, doing what comes naturally and not striving very earnestly to do much more. There are long-gone .230 hitters pumping gas somewhere along Route 66 and perpetuating the cliché that Aaron "falls asleep at the plate, but then he hits the pitch right out of the catcher's mitt." Instinct it's got to be—and those wrists. How else could a guy be .320 lifetime (highest among active players with five years or more) with a swing that would get a kid cut from a high school team?

"Most guys couldn't hit the way I do," Aaron says with an objectivity that precludes false modesty. "I'm fortunate that all the things you have to do in baseball come naturally to me. I do have a hitch in my swing, and I hit off the front foot. I've seen the movies. The weight is forward, but you notice the hands are always back. If they throw me a changeup I'm not out in front. I can adjust.

"I know, they think I don't care. I look like I'm running easy to first base, but I'm watching the outfielder, and if he messes up I can accelerate—I have the speed to shift gears."

In the eighth inning of a game at Los Angeles, Dodgers rightfielder Lou Johnson galloped to the railing and watched a foul ball land 20 rows in the stands. In the home half of the inning rightfielder Aaron took three steps and watched a foul ball land seven rows in. "I knew it was in the stands," Henry said. "What would it prove to run over there? That's false hustle. I hustle when I have to."

Like DiMaggio. Sangfroid, and all that? Not quite. "You ever notice," Henry asked, "that sometimes just before I step in the box I take a deep breath? I have to do that to get loose. I don't mean I'm tense, exactly, but I always have something on my mind. I have to study this game all the time and concentrate. There are things I've learned about pitchers, and I have tried to tell the younger players. But most of them can't see what I see, because they haven't concentrated and studied.

"I always talk to the kids, though, because you can learn from them. Maybe Maury Wills couldn't teach you about baserunning, just because he knows it so well it's hard for him to convey the idea. But you might hear something from some young player that would be valuable—something you never thought of."

At the Los Angeles airport Henry listened attentively to a lecture from teammate Gary Geiger on sliding. Aaron's take-off, Geiger suggested, was too late. At 29, Geiger is no longer a kid, but a frustrating succession of injuries and illness have limited his experience. "Well, what kind of slide do you think is best?" Henry asked, and held still for the answer. The computer mind was filing the data for evaluation.

The airport discussion of baserunning mistakes had broadened into a seminar on baseball mistakes in general, when the Braves' players discovered a celebrity in their midst. The golfer Phil Rodgers had just arrived from England and was liquidating some of his $1,949 booty from the British Open. He was introduced around, and the talk turned to golf. There may be more golf nuts per capita among baseball players than among any splinter group of American society, and Henry Aaron is one of them. Able to play only a couple of months a year, he has shot a 75. He shook hands with Rodgers and said it was nice to meet him. "But what I mean is. . . . " he said, and resumed the baseball talk.

In the fifth inning that afternoon, with Joe Torre on first base, Mike de la Hoz had singled to centerfield. The Dodgers' Willie Davis, characteristically, had thrown high over the cutoff man's head in an unsuccessful attempt to get Torre at third. "Mike should have taken second," Aaron said. "You have to anticipate that the outfielder will goof up one way or another."

Mike scored anyway, and the Braves won. Otherwise Aaron wouldn't have broached the subject, because he played under Ben Garaghty at Jacksonville in 1953. "I had a hell of a year," Henry said, "but one day I stole second three times. Each time I left the bag before the second baseman gave the ball back to the pitcher, and each time I was tagged out. He really chewed me.

"Ben never said anything after we lost, but if we made mistakes in a game we won we'd hear about them. He was the best manager I ever played for." (In 13 big league seasons Aaron has played for Charlie Grimm, Fred Haney, Charlie Dressen, Birdie Tebbetts and Bobby Bragan, who among them managed 10 big league teams and won five pennants.)

On the plane to the All-Star Game in St. Louis, the passengers had finished their complimentary cocktail and their glass of champagne, and two of them approached Aaron with paper and ballpoint pen. They were longtime admirers of his, and would he please sign this for the kid? "What's his name?" Henry asked, then inscribed best wishes to Danny. The two guys said they were from Tupelo, Miss., and that they hoped Hank would really tear up that American League tomorrow. He said thank you.

"Yeah, I remember Tupelo," Henry said later. "I drove through there a few years ago in a brand-new Oldsmobile." A Negro, and a very dark Negro at that, driving through Tupelo, Miss., in a shiny new Oldsmobile. "A cop got behind me when I crossed the city line, and he rode on my tail all the way to the other city line. I remember Tupelo, all right."

AARON IS aware that in the past decade he has enjoyed the insulation of prominence—but he hasn't enjoyed it. "They don't give me a bad time, because I'm somebody special. But that doesn't help my brothers and sisters, and anything that happens to any member of my race happens to me. I know how it feels, because sometimes people don't know who I am. The South doesn't have any monopoly on prejudice. At least the people in Mississippi have the guts to tell you they don't like you, and you know what to expect. But in the North they do it differently. I went into a restaurant in New York City one afternoon, and they wouldn't serve me. They didn't say they wouldn't, they just left me sitting there."

Aaron was born in Down the Bay, a Negro district of Mobile. It isn't at all down the bay, and nobody remembers why it was called that. Thus nobody knows exactly why the kids of Down the Bay considered themselves superior to those of Toulminville, an outer district where Henry's father moved his wife and eight children. This was the first discrimination Henry ever knew. "It wasn't white to black," he says. "It was black to black. They just thought they were better than we were. Anyway, it cost me my first chance at a big league tryout."

Neither Central High School, where Henry went for a while, nor Josephine Allen, the private school where he finished, had a baseball team. The emphasis was on football, so he played halfback and end. "I was pretty good," Henry says, "but I didn't especially like the game." He played on the schools' softball teams, and by the time he was 15 he was playing infield and hitting cross-handed for the Mobile Bears, a sand-lot club. "Sometimes on Sunday I'd make five or six dollars."

The Dodgers held an annual tryout camp in Mobile, one of those cursory ones in which a scout watches each kid pick up a few ground balls before telling him he can go. "When it came my turn," Henry says, "some big kid from Down the Bay pushed me aside, so I never got a chance."

Occasionally the kids from Toulminville would tire of being upstaged, and there would be a gang fight, but young Henry never was involved. "I don't want to brag," he says, "but I've never been in trouble. My mother would tell you I always was a sort of mature kid. I guess it was because I've always been a loner. Even in the big leagues, except when Bill Bruton was my roommate, I've kept pretty much to myself."

When Aaron reached St. Louis a man approached him and asked if, on his next trip in, he would talk to a Negro group, largely kids, and Henry said he would. As strong as his feelings on civil rights are, a membership in the NAACP is the extent of his active participation. "I'm approached all the time," he says, "but I feel that the only effective movements are the nonviolent movements, and I can't guarantee nonviolence. I don't feel nonviolent about it."

A white man found this out one day when he questioned the right of Aaron and several other Negro ballplayers to stand and talk on the sidewalk in front of a Tampa hotel. A Negro teammate found it out in the Braves' dressing room when he tested the theory that it is "in" for one Negro to apply racial epithets to another. Aaron will testify in no precise details to either incident, but he concedes that in each case his resistance was definitely not passive.

It is unlikely that Henry will ever apply for a Georgia real-estate license, although he has been pleasantly surprised by Atlanta. Life at 519 Lynnhurst Drive, on two rolling, shaded acres of grass and in a comfortable brick ranch house, has been as idyllic as air conditioning can make it. Barbara finds food prices high, but racial tensions are uncommonly low in this most cosmopolitan of cities below the Mason-Dixon line.

Two-acre plots considerably diminish the significance of racial composition but, for the record, Lynnhurst Drive is a mixed community.

"Yes, I was disturbed last year about the move to Atlanta," Henry says, "but the racial situation was a minor factor. We were happy in Milwaukee. I've never found a better place to bring up kids. There are so many different things to do."

Such as parks and beaches and things for the kids. And for Henry, the kid from Down the Bay who had found a way of life in Milwaukee, there were handball games at the firehouse, golf on the municipal courses and a quick ride to Chicago to catch Sammy Davis Jr. or a musical fresh out of New York. And, most of all, there was the civic embrace of Milwaukee fans in those first few years, the most aggressive acceptance a baseball team has ever known. "The fans here in Atlanta have been great," Aaron says, "especially the way we've been going. They haven't ever booed anybody but the manager. But—and I don't care how many people they draw in Los Angeles—there never will be anything like the way they treated us in Milwaukee in the early '50s."

"That's Hankie," Dorinda said, pointing to a picture in the family snapshot album, "and Larry. They go to camp. Gail goes to camp too." And Dorinda will go to camp. Henry Jr., 9, and Larry, 8, would play baseball all day if their mother didn't call a halt. "But I want them to be interested in other things," Henry said. "I wouldn't mind their being ballplayers, but only under one condition: They have to be good ballplayers. I've seen too many guys go up and down. I think it hurt my brother that his name was the same as mine. People expected things of him that he just couldn't do. I don't want my kids to have to face that kind of pressure." (Tommie Aaron, now 27 and playing for Richmond in the International League, still is an unquestioned artist as a first baseman-outfielder. But in two seasons with the Braves he had a .222 average and was gone.)

Gail, 11, will go to college first. "I want my kids to have the chances I never had," Aaron says. "My father was a welder in a shipyard, and he couldn't do it. He made a living, but he had to make ends meet, week to week, in those days. I think he did pretty well to put three kids through college." Herbert Aaron, now "about 65," did very well, but he has had a little help putting Henry's youngest sister through Florida A&M. After the 1959 season there was a short-lived television production called Home Run Derby, and Henry Aaron hit more balls out of cozy little Wrigley Field in Los Angeles than anybody else. For this he won $13,500, and with it he acquired a grocery store and two houses on Andrews Street in Mobile. His father has been operating the grocery store ever since.

"I'm not laying out any program for my kids," Henry says. "I want them to be what they want to be. I've seen people decide they want their kid to be a doctor or something. Then the kid changes his mind, and it's like an explosion in his parents' life. I just want them to have the chance."

The chance is further insured by another 50 or 75 acres of property 10 miles outside the Mobile city limits. Most of the real estate Aaron owns is either dormant or in a break-even rental status now, but he believes he will activate it when he's through playing.

"Real estate is the thing I know, outside of baseball," Henry says, "but I'm not thinking about that now. I want to play as long as I can, but I want to quit before I become a burden. I don't want to stay too long. It's a great thing to go out of this game gracefully."

IT WOULD be another great thing to reach 3,000 hits, joining a select company that just eluded Rogers Hornsby and Willie Keeler, and Henry will pass the 2,400 plateau in late August. "That's my goal," he says. "If I make that, I figure the other things will fall in place." Some home runs will fall in, as 424 had by this year's All-Star break. Babe Ruth's record 714 is remote, but there are those who expect 200 more home runs of Willie Mays, who is 35. It is hardly less realistic to expect 300 more from Aaron, who is 32.

Aaron has hit three homers in a game and 45 in a season, but one stands out in his memory. The score was 2–2 in the 11th inning at Milwaukee on the night of Sept. 23, 1957, and the magic number for Milwaukee's first pennant was 1. Billy Muffett, a curveballer, was pitching for the Cardinals, and he hadn't served up a home run all season. He threw a curve, Bad Henry swung, Wally Moon went back to the 402-foot sign in centerfield and jumped, and urchins who should have been home in bed scrambled for the ball in front of the cedar trees. Braves general manager John Quinn and a cast of thousands burst into tears of joy.

For several seconds of Milwaukee's finest hour Henry Aaron wasn't there. Running between second and third base he was back on Edwards Avenue in Mobile, on his way home from school. The day was Oct. 3, 1951. Henry had just heard on somebody's radio that Bobby Thomson had homered to win a pennant, and he ran the rest of the way, giving a little leap every few steps as Thomson did. The cross-handed-hitting Negro sandlotter from Toulminville was Bobby Thomson that day, and he was again that night in Milwaukee, until he rounded third, saw the reception committee and knew it was at least as much fun to be Henry Aaron.

◇

POSTSCRIPT: *Though he hit only .279, the lowest average in his 13 seasons in the bigs to that point, Aaron would end 1966 with 44 homers, and 442 overall. If Aaron was not yet considered a serious threat to Babe Ruth's record of 714, it was due, in part, to his gradual-ist approach to accumulating homers. In addition to his 60-home run season in 1927, Ruth had eclipsed the 50-mark three other times. Even Mantle and Mays had reached the plateau twice; Aaron would not fin-ish with more than 47 in a season. Of Aaron's career, SI's Ron Fimrite wrote in 1994, "Consistency was Aaron's game, not theatricality."*

◇

Hank Becomes
A Hit

BY WILLIAM LEGGETT

*A rare Braves pennant drive lifted the Hammer from
relative obscurity to fame at long last*

THERE IS A WARM, PLEASING UNDERCURRENT MAKING
its way through the world of baseball. It flows from the
Western Division of the National League, where a stimulating
pennant race involving not two clubs, nor three, but five—
count 'em!—is adding meaning to every move that the players
make before the nervous eyes of their hopeful fans. The source
of this undercurrent is Henry Aaron of the Atlanta Braves,
who suddenly this August is attracting the attention that
his exploits have merited for years. Not long ago, in
Montreal's Jarry Park, a startled Aaron found himself the
object of a standing ovation when his name was announced—
in French. Each time Aaron came to bat before a tumultuous
crowd of 43,000 in Atlanta Stadium on Aug. 8 the applause
increased. When on the next day he hit the 539th major
league home run of his career the din was enormous. A day
later, as New York pitchers carefully walked him twice in a

tight ball game, there it was, louder still: noise, enthusiasm, recognition. Sportswriters and announcers are approaching Aaron as never before, and people are standing outside club-house entrances to stretch for the autograph or touch the sleeve of a man who is doing no more and no less than he has for most of his 16 years in the major leagues.

It seems that a vast subconscious wrong is being righted and that in the remaining weeks of this season and at least into the next one Henry Aaron, an all-but-anonymous star, is going to be one of the most closely watched players in baseball.

One reason for the attention is that Aaron is chasing two tremendous baseball records simultaneously: 3,000 hits and a possibility of passing Babe Whatsisname as the alltime home run hitter. Since he is now 35, it is doubtful that Aaron will stay around long enough to hit the 176 homers he needs to pass Ruth, but attaining his 3,000th base hit is almost a cer-tainty, and only eight men have ever done that.

This year Aaron has been passing baseball's records as if they were painted on a post. He has now gone to the plate more than 9,000 times, hit for more than 5,000 total bases and collected over 500 doubles. Since April he has passed Mel Ott, Eddie Mathews, Ted Williams, Jimmy Foxx and Mickey Mantle on the alltime home run list. Only Willie Mays, with 596, stands between Aaron's 539 and the 714 of Ruth.

Despite his ability, longevity, consistency and willingness to play even when injured, the fame that was accorded Mantle, Mays and Musial has never been granted to Aaron. This year Mantle himself has said he believes Aaron to be the most underrated great hitter of all time. For his part, Aaron concludes it is youngsters who have appreciated him most over the years, because "adults tend to just read the headlines sometimes. Kids read everything, all the way down through the box scores and the statistics."

But the mood is changing. In recent weeks the public—young and old—is beginning to recognize Henry Aaron. "I feel it now and hear it," says Atlanta third baseman Clete Boyer, who was with the Yankees and Mantle for eight seasons.

"It's starting to get like it was for Mickey. And it's only right. Henry knows more baseball than any man I have ever met. Maybe the fact that he was colored hurt him in getting publicity, but maybe the fact that he is colored has helped him to understand people more than any other player I have known. He's not a pop-off. If he wanted to manage I know that he could do it. If he was a manager he would be a lot like [the Dodgers' Walter] Alston, and Alston is the very best."

He is the same Aaron that players have held in awe for years. His quick wrists still snap the bat around with tremendous speed, and he hits what are known in baseball's dugouts as "frozen ropes." He is the most consistent player in a game that demands consistency of its genuine heroes. His record in this respect is remarkable. Only once did he fail to hit .280. That was in 1966, the year the Braves made their move from Milwaukee to Atlanta. His average fell that year to .279, but with 44 home runs and 127 runs batted in, nobody could complain that his hitting was inadequate.

Because of his consistency and high level of performance in

so many categories, an average season for him produces eye-opening statistics. And when 16 such years are run together, it is no wonder that he is ranked among the greatest.

"People keep wondering if I will be around long enough to break Babe Ruth's home run record," Aaron says. "I really don't know. I do know that I will not hang on just for the sake of hanging on—picking up 12 one year and maybe 20 the next and jumping from club to club. I have too much respect for the game of baseball to do that just to chase someone's record.

"When I came into baseball I had a taste for it in my mouth and that has never changed. I still love to play, though it gets harder with the length of the schedule, the traveling and the night games. Often the fans don't realize what a player must go through and how tired he can get. But the fan is the one who pays his money, and he expects to receive the best for it. He goes to games to see people like Sandy Koufax pitch and Maury Wills steal bases; to see Willie Mays make the basket catch and Henry Aaron hit. When I don't hit I feel bad about it, because the fans might feel cheated. It bothers you if you are a professional."

Bill Bartholomay, for one, has never felt cheated. As he sat in his office last week as that crowd of 43,000 started to enter the stadium for a twi-night double-header, the president of the Braves reflected about Aaron.

"One of the few right things I might have done in Milwaukee was to get to know Aaron right away," Bartholomay said. "My admiration for him goes beyond description. He's Mr. Brave. We are not going to press Henry to hang on for public relations reasons. It's up to Henry to make his own decision on when he wants to stop playing. If he wants to stay on the field as a coach or a manager that's up to him, or if he wants to come into the front office that is open to him, too. Any route he decides to take will have my full support. All Henry will have to do is tell us."

And minutes later the Atlanta crowd was cheering its Hank. Recognition had come. There was even proof of it. In two categories of baseball's alltime statistics—total hits and runs batted in—Aaron is running neck and neck with Willie Mays. Three weeks ago burglars broke into the home of Tal Smith, director of player personnel of the Houston Astros. Smith had two autographed baseballs mounted side by side. One was signed by Willie Mays, the other by Henry Aaron. The Aaron ball was stolen. The Mays ball was not. Henry, you're finally famous!

◇

POSTSCRIPT: *The Braves would edge out Mays's Giants to win the inaugural NL West title. Despite a homer in each game from Aaron, the Braves were swept by the eventual champion Mets in what would be Aaron's final postseason appearance. For the sixth time in his career, Aaron broke the 40-homer barrier, hitting 44 to bring his lifetime output to 554, still 160 short of the Babe. In the coming years, for the first time, the possibility of a new home run king would start to take hold. For Aaron, the best—and alas, the worst—was yet to come.*

◇

The First Frontier

BY WILLIAM LEGGETT

*Number 714 was still a distant dream on May 17, 1970,
when Aaron reached another milestone: 3,000 hits*

"IT WAS GETTING AWFULLY LONELY IN THE CLUB," STAN Musial was saying recently in Cincinnati, "and when you are the only living member of it, you wait around for somebody to join you so at least there will be somebody to talk to."

In the second game of a May 17 doubleheader between the Reds and the Atlanta Braves in Crosley Field, Henry Aaron beat out an infield single and joined Musial and seven others in baseball history to reach 3,000 hits. Musial vaulted over the small fence alongside the Braves' dugout and trotted out to first to congratulate Aaron, as the biggest Cincinnati crowd in 23 years gave the game's most underpublicized star a heartfelt standing ovation. Aaron held up the ball that he had hit off rookie pitcher Wayne Simpson and waved it at the big crowd.

"Congratulations, Henry," said Musial.

"Thank you so much for coming over to see me do it."

Aaron's single drove in a run for the Braves in their big

showdown series with the Reds. Not long after, on his way to downtown Cincinnati in a police car, Musial said, "Sure I remember my 3,001st hit. It was a home run." No sooner were the words out of his mouth than a radio broadcast told the story of No. 3,001 for Aaron. It was a home run over the centerfield fence. "Go get 'em, Henry," said Musial.

Aaron had been trying to join Cap Anson (1897), Honus Wagner and Nap Lajoie (both 1914), Ty Cobb ('21), Tris Speaker and Eddie Collins (both '25), Paul Waner ('42) and Musial ('58) in the 3,000-hit club. Lou Gehrig never reached the plateau and Babe Ruth retired 127 hits short of it. George Sisler, with a lifetime batting average of .340, did not get 3,000 hits, nor did Ted Williams, Joe DiMaggio, Harry Heilmann, Wee Willie Keeler, Kiki Cuyler, Rogers Hornsby, Mel Ott, Ducky Medwick, Sam Rice, Al Simmons or Heinie Manush. Mickey Mantle never really got close, and Willie Mays is still 43 away.

Getting 3,000 hits is baseball's finest unsung record, but Aaron approached his goal without fanfare or trumpets from Major League Baseball Commissioner Bowie Kuhn or National League president Charles Feeney. The fans, fortunately, responded to him. After doubling twice to move within one hit of 3,000, Aaron sat in front of his locker in the Braves' clubhouse in Cincinnati and said wistfully, "People have been calling me on the phone and wishing me the best of luck. I appreciate it very much. It's very nice to know that people know you are around."

Opposing pitchers certainly know he's been around. Fear of

Hank Aaron has been present in baseball for most of the past 16 seasons. Now, in his 17th season, that fear is larger than it has ever been before. On opening night in Atlanta 37,181 fans watched him come to bat in the first inning and pump a home run 503 feet into the upper deck in leftfield. It was the longest homer ever hit by a Brave in Atlanta.

"Throwing a fastball by Henry Aaron," pitcher Curt Simmons once said, "is like trying to sneak the sun past a rooster."

At an age—36—when other ballplayers are beginning to enjoy the twilight of their careers, Aaron is now in the first year of a two-year contract that calls for $125,000 a year. He lacks only a few things that he wants and once had. "There was a fire in my home in Atlanta three years ago," he said recently, "and some of the things I really treasured were lost, like the balls I hit for my 1,000th and 2,000th hits. I wonder if my 3,000th hit is a homer if I'll get it back."(It wasn't and, of course, he did.)

As Aaron moved toward 3,000, some of baseball's biggest names watched him and appreciated the milestone he was approaching. Ernie Banks, who himself just became only the ninth man in baseball to hit 500 homers, sat on the edge of the Chicago dugout and said, "How do you pitch to a hammer? What does he think about when the count is three and one? Does he feel that he has to carry the team? Does he realize that he makes hitting with two strikes on him look easy while the rest of us normal people tense up? I was impressed when I first saw him hit, and I'm more impressed by Mr. Henry Aaron as the years roll by."

Red Schoendienst, the manager of the Cardinals and a

teammate of both Aaron and Musial, as well as one of the 111 others in baseball to collect more than 2,000 hits, says, "Two thousand hits is nothing when you compare it to 3,000. When I played with Henry in Milwaukee I thought he would have a chance to reach 3,000 hits because he had the perfect body that would allow him to play every day. Good hitters just play, and bad hitters become politicians and try to hang on that way. Henry's just like Stan; both are natural-born hitters. They began to concentrate when they got to the clubhouse and they would look at the laces when they tied their shoes because they knew that once their shoes were on, they had to play. No distractions. No horsefeathers, just work. That's what makes a real man. That was Stan, and it's Henry."

"Henry could steal 50 bases a year if he wanted to and seldom get caught," says Roger Maris, "but he knows that he might get hurt, and that would harm his ballclub in the long run. In some ways it is unfortunate that Henry's hitting is so outstanding. It tends to overshadow his other talents."

Joe Torre played with Aaron in both Milwaukee and Atlanta and now must play against him as a Cardinal. "Henry," he says, "has the most ferocious swing with the least amount of effort that I have ever seen. He can hit a ball in the infield and judge how much speed to turn on to beat the throw. The old saying applies to Henry. He belongs in a higher league."

So, of course, did the other 3,000-hit men. One of them, Waner, was the team's batting instructor when Aaron was in his fourth year as a Milwaukee Brave, and a bright enough man to leave Aaron's style alone. "We talked about hitting quite a bit," Aaron said while lounging in his Cincinnati hotel room in scarlet silk pajamas, "and our theories were almost the same. Waner believed, as I do, that moving the legs or opening and closing your stance is not as important as the upper part on the body. It's the controlling of the bat that is important and being able to snap your wrists at the last instant that allows you to do something with a pitch you might have already been fooled on."

Waner got his 3,000th hit at the age of 39. With 2,999 to his credit, he hit a ground ball that shortstop Eddie Joost could not field cleanly. It seemed that Waner's 3,000th hit would be a scratch single. When he got to first base, however, Waner motioned with his arms and head "no" to the official scorer. Reluctantly, the scorer called the play an error and Waner later told Joost, "I'm sorry to see you get an error, kid, but I wanted it to be one I could be proud of." Eventually Waner did get his hit—a single through the middle against the Pirates, his old team. Although Waner was nearing the end of a career in which his top salary was $18,500, he volunteered to put up $1,000 for a celebration party. But his hard-up employers, the Braves, stepped in and paid.

Musial, who flew to Cincinnati to be there for Aaron's historic hit, had two parties for his 3,000th, the first when he reached 2,998 before the team went to Chicago for a short series. Musial hoped the second would be in St. Louis, too. With one hit to go, he sat out the last Chicago game before returning home. He was sunning himself in the bullpen in the sixth inning when, with the Cardinals behind 3–1, manager Fred Hutchinson summoned him to pinch-hit for Sad Sam Jones. Musial doubled to drive in a run, and the Cards went on to win.

Following his hit, photographers ran onto the field, the ball was presented to Musial, and Hutchinson took him out of the game for a pinch runner. Musial ran over to the box seats, hugged and kissed his wife, and one of the photographers asked, "Say, Stan, did you know that blonde?"

The Cardinals returned by train to St. Louis—the last train trip in the club's history. In Clinton, Ill., a crowd of about 50 gathered on the station platform and chanted, "We want Musial." At Springfield the crowd had doubled, and people were singing, "For he's a jolly good fellow." When the train pulled into Union Station a spotlight was put on Musial. "I never realized," he told a huge crowd, "that batting a little white ball around would cause so much commotion. I know now how Lindbergh must have felt when he returned to St . Louis."

Aaron's first game in the majors was played in Crosley Field, the site of his 3,000th hit. He got no hits in five at bats. Joe Nuxhall was the starting pitcher that day for the Reds, and all he recalls of Aaron at the time was, "In the clubhouse meeting before the game he was thought to be a high-ball hitter." The Braves returned to Milwaukee after their Opening Day loss for an opener against the Cardinals and Aaron's second game in the majors. Vic Raschi, ending his career, was the starting pitcher for St. Louis. "Nobody on our team seemed to know anything about Aaron," Raschi says, "except Eddie Stanky, the manager. He knew that Aaron was a potentially fine player and talked about everything except the way Henry parted his hair."

On his first at bat in County Stadium Aaron doubled off the leftfield wall. Not long afterward he launched the first homer of his remarkable career—this one off Raschi in St. Louis.

Aaron is the first man ever to combine 3,000 hits and 500 home runs. Assuming that an average Aaron home run travels only 340 feet, he has already hit more than 36½ miles worth. Many people believe that he has a good chance to reach Babe Ruth's alltime record of 714. "This year and the next are the critical ones for me if I am going to catch Ruth," Aaron says. "I would almost have to have a 50-homer year in one of the two seasons. One reason I have gotten off so fast is that Rico Carty and Orlando Cepeda have been hitting behind me. They've been going real good, so I have been getting more pitches to hit. Sure, catching Ruth would be a thrill, but achieving 3,000 hits is more important because it shows consistency. I have studied the list of men who reached 3,000, and the most remarkable one is Ty Cobb because he got to 4,191. That is unbelievable to me." If Henry Aaron has a few more seasons like this one, he could become a believer.

◇

POSTSCRIPT: *For Aaron the hits would keep coming—at an especially furious pace for a man fast approaching 40. Thirty-eight home runs in 1970, a career-high 47 (in fewer than 500 at bats) the following year. By the start of the '73 season, Aaron would stand at 663 homers, only 51 short of the Babe. But amid the anticipation of the chase were the first visible hints of the torment, a virulence that Aaron would not fully acknowledge in public for several years.*

◇

THE CHASE

◇

The Torturous
Road to 715

BY WILLIAM LEGGETT

As the Home Run King–in-Waiting swung toward a
magical number, the reality of racism escalated

THE IMMORTAL HENRY AARON, TO COIN A PHRASE, WAS sitting quietly in the visitors' dugout at the Astrodome in Houston, preparing himself for another evening of being chased by Babe Ruth's ghost. He looked out at the pitcher's mound, where an overweight man in his late 30s was throwing batting practice to the Astros. "Turk Farrell," said Aaron. "Haven't seen him in a few years. I didn't know he worked batting practice for them. Had real good stuff." Aaron put his hands behind his head, leaned his shoulders against the wall and spoke what was really on his mind. "Babe. Babe. Babe. Babe. Babe Ruth. I never made a study of the man, but I know an awful lot about him. It seems that everybody I talk to tells me a little bit more."

Is this to be the year in which Aaron, at the age of 39, takes a moon walk above one of the most hallowed individual records in American sport, the 714 home runs struck by George

Herman Ruth? Or will it be remembered as the season in which Aaron, the most dignified of athletes, was besieged with hate mail and trapped by the cobwebs and goblins that lurk in baseball's attic? As the season began, Aaron needed 41 homers to tie Ruth, 42 to top him. And what a start he has made. On May 13, in a Sunday doubleheader against the San Diego Padres in Atlanta, he pinch-hit a home run, only his third in a pinch-hit role in 20 years, and he added another homer in the second game. Already he is several days ahead of Roger Maris's pace toward the Ruth-surpassing number 61 in 1961.

"I was reading the morning paper over a cup of coffee the day after Aaron got two," Maris says, "and when I realized that he had 10, I thought to myself, that's a lot for this early in the season for a guy 39 years old. Whenever people ask me about Henry's chances of breaking the record I tell them that because of his great swing and attitude, he should do it. I don't see how he can miss. But the pressures are going to grow. I hope the public will realize that he is just a man trying to do a job."

But Aaron is doing far more than a job. Rarely a day passes that this grand warrior does not make news. His statistical accomplishments are so vast and continuous that putting them into perspective is as difficult as standing at the depot and trying to remember freight car numbers as they pass. Aaron recently went to bat for the 11,000th time; only Ty Cobb remains ahead of him in that category (11,429). He also scored the 2,000th run of his career, something achieved previously by only three others. It won't be long before he surpasses Ruth and Stan Musial in extra-base hits (Musial had 1,377, Ruth 1,356).

And he also will become the premier righthanded hitter of all time when he tops 3,431 hits, the record held by Honus Wagner.

As impressive as all those accomplishments are and will be, the big number is 715. The very enormousness of it is closing in fast on Aaron, both on and off the field. In the first 25 games of 1973 Aaron was walked 22 times because, frankly, the pitchers are afraid of him. Enemy infields overshift, trying to force him to hit to rightfield. But Aaron ignores them and takes the overhead route—to use the baseball vernacular, "goes for the pump." His average has slipped, but the home runs keep coming—of his first 25 hits, 11 were homers.

Some say there is evidence of the increasing pressure in the number of times Aaron steps out of the batter's box, how tightly he seems to be holding his bat, the way he questions umpires about strikes. But when Babe Ruth is chasing you, people see a lot of things they never took time to notice before. And, yes, it is a matter of Ruth chasing Aaron, the old legends dogging his steps, wraiths in pinstripes hounding him at every turn.

ALWAYS ONE to read his fan mail and answer it, Aaron has found that while the overwhelming majority of letter writers are on his side, an inordinate number do not want him to get No. 715. For a few of those who wish him ill, the reason is that Ruth is a hallowed figure in their pantheon. For most, his blackness is sufficient to denigrate his quest. Letters sent to Aaron in the past were filled with charm and gratitude: "My dog loves you. When my dad watches one of your games, she sits up and wags her tail hard." And: "One time my brother and a friend of ours were playing ball and I hit it and was going to third base and slid and the base went up in the air. My brother came up and tagged the base. Was I safe?" And: "Could you send a Braves scout down [to Augusta]? There is a boy in my class who can hit home runs every time he gets to bat." He seemed to have no undue difficulties in Atlanta.

But now many of his letters start with the salutation, "Dear Nigger," and go downhill from there. "It bothers me," says Aaron. "I have seen a President shot and his brother shot. The man who murdered Dr. Martin Luther King is in jail, but that isn't doing Dr. King much good, is it? I have four children and I have to be concerned about their welfare."

In a recent week more than 2,000 letters to Aaron were received at Atlanta Stadium. More arrive at his home. The volume is so great that the club has assigned Aaron a secretary, Carla Koplin, to handle the mail. She sits with stacks of it, opening it, sorting it, wishing that Aaron would read less of it. But Aaron reads and reads.

At 190 pounds Aaron is only 10 pounds heavier than when he first came out of Jacksonville 20 years ago and got a job with the Braves, then in Milwaukee, because Bobby Thomson broke an ankle in a spring-training slide. Aaron's wrists still have the quickness that enables him to flick his bat out and snap the outside pitch to leftfield, but the Aaron arm is not what it used to be. "It hurts at times," he says. This season he was moved from rightfield to left so that runners could not spin so easily from first to third on singles to right or score from second without a challenge. "I went to Aaron," says man-

ager Eddie Mathews, "and said, 'Henry, what do you think
about moving over to left?' He just said, 'Yes.' "

As for the legs, well, how many power hitters could run like
Aaron to start with? At the age of 34 he stole 28 bases in 33
attempts, but such seasons are now just memories and
Mathews has put pinch runners in for him in the late innings
of some games.

But it is the bat, of course, that counts now. Unlike most aging
hitters, Aaron can still handle the fastball—on those rare occasions when he sees one. "Once in a while, when a pitcher thinks
I'm tired, he might throw one," Aaron says. These days they try
to fool him with breaking pitches, but they still get burned
unless the pitches are superior. Claude Osteen of the Dodgers,
Aaron's No. 1 home run victim among active pitchers (he has
given up 13), says, "Slapping a rattlesnake across the face with
the back of your hand is safer than trying to fool Henry Aaron."

Aaron knows the strike zone down to the last millimeter,
and he has great patience. He will wait for his pitch and then
crush it. For years he sprayed the ball hard to all fields, but in
recent seasons he has become a pull hitter. Most National
League teams now put three men on the third-base side of the
infield against him to stop balls from going through. They also
bunch their outfields by moving the centerfielder over into left
and the rightfielder toward center. The right side of the infield
is open, of course, but few hitters can steer a pitched ball well
enough to roll it through. Aaron is not asked to try.

"I know what it's like to be shifted against," says Mathews,
who holds the record for most homers by a third baseman

(483). "It was done to me. You just don't change a man of 39 who has meant to this game what Henry means. Henry went to camp this spring and worked his tail off. There were times when I had to stop him because I thought he might be overextending himself. The strain on him is going to be enormous as the season progresses, but we are going to do everything possible to help him. It's because of who he is chasing that the pressure will build. Heck, when he and I combined for most home runs hit by teammates, there was no pressure at all. We didn't even know we were going after the record until a month after we had broken it."

Ruth's revered 714 seems to possess a majesty so great that it might have come to us engraved on a stone tablet, but whose record did Ruth break? Nobody really knows. Going into the 1921 season, Gavvy Cravath appeared to hold it with 117 homers to Ruth's 103. But when Ruth hit No. 117 *The New York Times* did not mention it. A week later *The Sporting News* smugly summed things up as follows: "Contrary to report, Babe Ruth did not equal Cravath's lifetime major league home run record when the slugging Babe smote a four-base lick off Dave Keefe of the Athletics on May 29. Cravath, who retired after 11 years in the majors with a record of hitting more home runs than any major-leaguer, has a total of 119 home runs to his credit, not 117 as some records show. He made two as an American Leaguer that had been overlooked."

Further research disclosed that 136 homers were hit by one Roger Connor from 1880 to '97, and two other players, Sam Thompson and Harry Stovey, also hit more than Cravath. But what Ruth did was unique, and he changed the game. Until Ruth began hitting homers the standard offense relied on the steal, the hit-and-run, singles and doubles. In 1915, Ruth's first full season, the Boston Red Sox won the American League pennant with a team total of 13 home runs. Pitcher Ruth (18–8) led his club with four and Braggo Roth topped the American League with seven. Three seasons later the whole American League amassed only 100 homers. Ruth, functioning as pitcher, outfielder and first baseman, tied for the major league lead with 11 homers. Again the Red Sox won the pennant; the rest of the team hit exactly five home runs.

In 1920 Ruth was sold to the Yankees for $125,000, the ball was given an injection of rabbit fluid, the spitball and other moist pitches were ruled illegal, and 369 homers were hit in the American League. Attendance in the league, 1,708,000 in 1918, soared to 5,084,000 in 1920. The Yankees, sharing the Polo Grounds with John McGraw's Giants, saw their own attendance skyrocket from 282,000 to 1,289,000 and base-ball's future was forever changed.

As Aaron moves on toward Ruth's record it will be argued that it is easier to hit homers today than it was then; that the fences Ruth was shooting at were more distant; that the pitch-ers today are not as good as they were then. But these are merely nontruths being handed down as gospel in the interest of keeping the glitter on glorious days. The fact is that the rightfield fence at the Polo Grounds was only 257 feet from home plate and the one at Yankee Stadium 296 feet. Balls that bounced over or through fences counted as homers. In the years Ruth played in the majors most of his homers came on the road (363 to 351), and no records were kept of balls bouncing into the seats. "When Babe hit them," says Leo Durocher, a man who played with some of his Yankee teams and recalls those times with ardor, "you had to have a good seat to get a ball. He hit them so far they didn't need any bounce on them to be homers. Babe Ruth was a fantastic hitter and so is Henry Aaron. He is the greatest righthanded hitter since Rogers Hornsby, and nobody will ever be better than Hornsby in my book."

Joe Monahan, chief scout for the St. Louis Cardinals, says, "I saw Ruth take batting practice a few times. Once you saw that you wondered why he didn't hit more home runs than he did. One ball would be just going over the fence, a second would be halfway there and the third would just be leaving his bat."

"Ruth hit balls so high," says Durocher, "that the infielders would lose sight of them, or gather under them, and when they dropped Ruth would be standing on third with a triple hit no farther than 15 feet beyond second base."

When Aaron hit 47 homers in 1971 and also batted .327, Atlanta rewarded him with a $200,000 salary. The baseball world looked upon it with disbelief. It was assumed there must be conditions in it based on his eventual topping of Ruth's record or, at the very least, attendance clauses.

Well, attendance at Braves home games would not earn Aaron much. Atlanta crowds are off sharply from last season, one in which the Braves drew a puny 753,000. It seems as if they love Aaron on the road (where the Hammer is attracting nearly twice as many fans per game in the early going) and are notably cool toward him at home. What will happen when he goes past 700 remains to be seen.

IT WAS in April 1954 that Aaron hit No. 1. (Dwight Eisenhower was President, and the McCarthy hearings gripped the nation, just to put things in historical perspective.) It came off Vic Raschi of the Cardinals in Aaron's seventh big-league game. No. 109, hit in the 11th inning of a 2–2 game with St. Louis, clinched Milwaukee's first pennant in 1957. The following evening Aaron delivered No. 110 and it accomplished two things: It was the first of his 14 career grand slams and it won him the first of four National League home run championships.

Homer No. 215 has received little attention, although Aaron maintains it is the only one he ever hit in genuine anger. The Braves were playing the Dodgers at County Stadium in Milwaukee with Stan Williams pitching for Los Angeles. Aaron had heard that Williams kept a picture of him taped above his locker and threw darts at it on the days he would be pitching to him. His first time up, Williams hit Aaron with a 3–1 pitch. Henry felt it was deliberate and shouted a few words at Williams. Dodger first baseman Gil Hodges tried to quiet Aaron, but as he took a short lead away from first Williams threw over—and hit Aaron again. "I got hit two times in one inning," Aaron says, smiling about it now. "I was burning. When I came up again I was still burning. I was furious. I homered off him."

Some historians believe that Aaron was deprived of one

homer he deserved. He had it taken away in 1965 in one of the oddest of baseball rulings. The Braves were playing the Cardinals, with Curt Simmons pitching for St. Louis. Simmons was Aaron's nemesis, the one man he could never seem to hit. Simmons threw changeups when Henry thought he would be throwing fastballs and fastballs when Henry thought he would be throwing changes. That night Aaron guessed changeup and turned out to be correct. He hit the ball and it soared up onto the rightfield roof in Busch Stadium. But umpire Chris Pelekoudas called Aaron out for stepping on home plate as he swung. Nobody is rooting more for Aaron not to stop at 713 or 714 than Chris Pelekoudas.

Aaron won't stop. No. 715 will be reached but one thing is certain—it won't come easy. His appetite for the Spanish, Polynesian and Chinese food he likes so much is fading. He turns the phone off in the suite the Braves supply him on the road in order to get the sleep he finds increasingly elusive. There are ghosts in pinstripes, and too many walks, and months of "Dear Nigger" before the great day comes.

$\diamond$

POSTSCRIPT: *Even as he continued to endure an onslaught of hate mail, Aaron also served as a small balm for a country still at war in Vietnam and in the midst of the Watergate scandal. The Braves would set an attendance record in '73 and Aaron would prove an even bigger draw on the road—with good reason. The eighth, and final, 40-home run season of his career placed Aaron a tantalizing one home run away from immortality at season's end, giving a nation (and plenty of pitchers) an entire winter to ponder when and where history might be made.*

In 1953 Braves farmhand Aaron helped integrate the Deep South's Sally League.

JOHN ZIMMERMAN

In '57, long before the chase, Bad Henry made a powerful statement by winning the MVP.

Aaron (in '55) won over teammates Spahn (center) and Chuck Tanner from the start.

Hank, six-month-old Henry Jr. and Barbara Aaron reveled in Milwaukee's first pennant.

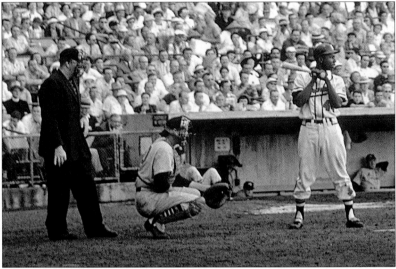

Aaron's cool, assured demeanor at the plate was often mistaken for indifference.

The Hammer was a thief too, stealing 240 bases in his career.

Aaron credited his parents, including dad, Herbert (in '69), for his social conscience.

Aaron (in '65) considered his years in Milwaukee as the happiest of his career.

Aaron and Mathews walked through their home tunnel for the final time as Milwaukee Braves.

In '69 the Greatest exchanged autographs with Atlanta's greatest at Dodger Stadium.

Even as he closed in on Ruth, Aaron remained a remarkably underpublicized figure.

◇

End of the
Glorious Ordeal

BY RON FIMRITE

Having gracefully endured the pressure of the Chase,
Aaron made history with one flick of his famous wrists

HENRY AARON'S ORDEAL ENDED AT 9:07 P.M., MONDAY, APRIL 8.

It ended in a carnival atmosphere that would have been more congenial to the man he surpassed as baseball's alltime home run champion. But it ended. And for that, as Aaron advised the 53,775 Atlanta fans who came to enshrine him in the game's pantheon, "Thank God."

Aaron's 715th home run came in the fourth inning of the Braves' home opener with Los Angeles, off the Dodgers' Al Downing, a lefthander who had insisted doggedly before the game that for him this night would be "no different from any other." He was wrong, for now he joins a company of victims that includes Tom Zachary (Babe Ruth's 60th home run in 1927), Tracy Stallard (Roger Maris's 61st in 1961) and Guy Bush (Ruth's 714th in 1935). They are destined to ride in tandem through history with their assailants.

Downing's momentous mistake was a high fastball into

Aaron's considerable strike zone. Aaron's whip of a bat lashed out at it and snapped it in a high arc toward the 385-foot sign in left centerfield. Dodger centerfielder Jimmy Wynn and left-fielder Bill Buckner gave futile chase, Buckner going all the way to the six-foot fence for it. But the ball dropped over the fence in the midst of a clutch of Braves' relief pitchers who scrambled out of the bullpen in pursuit. Buckner started to go over the fence after the ball himself, but gave up after he realized he was outnumbered. It was finally retrieved by reliever Tom House, who even as Aaron triumphantly rounded the bases ran hysterically toward home plate holding the ball aloft. It was, after all, one more ball than Babe Ruth ever hit over a fence, and House is a man with a sense of history.

House arrived in time to join a riotous spectacle at the plate. Aaron, his normally placid features exploding in a smile, was hoisted by his teammates as Downing and the Dodger infielders moved politely to one side. Aaron shook hands with his father Herbert, and embraced his mother Estella. He graciously accepted encomiums from his boss, Braves board chairman Bill Bartholomay, and Monte Irvin, representing Commissioner Bowie Kuhn, who was unaccountably in Cleveland this eventful night. Kuhn is no favorite of Atlanta fans and when his name was mentioned by Irvin, the largest crowd ever to see a baseball game in Atlanta booed lustily.

"I just thank God it's all over," said Aaron, giving credit where it is not entirely due.

No, this was Henry Aaron's evening, and if the Braves' management overdid it a bit with the balloons, the fireworks, the speeches and all-round hoopla, who is to quibble? There have not been many big baseball nights in this football-oriented community and those few have been supplied by Aaron.

Before the game the great man did look a trifle uncomfortable while being escorted through lines of majorettes as balloons rose in the air above him. There were signs everywhere—MOVE OVER BABE—and the electronic scoreboard blinked HANK. Much of centerfield was occupied by a massive map of the United States painted on the grass as an American flag. This map-flag was the site of a pregame *This Is Your Life* show, featuring Aaron's relatives, friends and employers. Sammy Davis Jr. was there, and Pearl Bailey, singing the national anthem in Broadway soul, and Atlanta's black mayor, Maynard Jackson, and Governor Jimmy Carter, and the Jonesboro High School band, and the Morris Brown College choir and Chief Noc-A-Homa, the Braves' mascot, who danced with a fiery hoop.

This is not the sort of party one gives for Henry Aaron, who through the long weeks of on-field pressure and mass media harassment had expressed no more agitation than a man brushing aside a housefly. Aaron had labored for most of his 21-year career in shadows cast by more flamboyant superstars, and if he was enjoying his newfound celebrity, he gave no hint of it. He seemed to be nothing more than a man trying to do his job and live a normal life in the presence of incessant chaos.

Before this most important game of his career he joked at

the batting cage with teammate Dusty Baker, a frequent foil, while hordes of newsmen scrambled around him, hanging on every banality. When a young red-haired boy impudently shouted, "Hey, Hank Aaron, come here, I want you to sign this," Aaron looked incredulous, then laughed easily. The poor youngster was very nearly mobbed by sycophants for approaching the dignitary so cavalierly.

Downing, too, seemed unaware that he was soon to be a party to history. "I will pitch to Aaron no differently tonight," he said as the band massed in rightfield. "I'll mix my pitches up, move the locations. If I make a mistake, it's no disgrace. I don't think the pitcher should take the glory for number 715. He won't deserve any accolades. I think people will remember the pitcher who throws the last one he ever hits, not the 715th."

Downing's "mistake" was made with nobody out in the fourth inning and with Darrell Evans, the man preceding Aaron in the Braves' batting order, on first base following an error by Dodger shortstop Bill Russell. Downing had walked Aaron leading off the second inning to the accompaniment of continuous booing by the multitudes. Aaron then scored on a Dodger error, the run breaking Willie Mays' alltime National League record for runs scored (after the home run, Aaron had 2,064).

This time, with a man on base, Downing elected to confront him *mano-a-mano*. His first pitch, however, hit the dirt in front of the plate. The next hit the turf beyond the fence in leftfield.

"It was a fastball down the middle of the upper part of the

plate," Downing lamented afterward. "I was trying to get it down to him, but I didn't. He's a great hitter. When he picks his pitch, he's pretty certain that's the pitch he's looking for. Chances are he's gonna hit it pretty good. When he did hit it, I didn't think it was going out because I was watching Wynn and Buckner. But the ball just kept carrying and carrying."

It was Aaron's first swing of the game—and perhaps the most significant in the history of baseball. It was also typical of Aaron's sense of economy. On Opening Day in Cincinnati, against the Reds' Jack Billingham, he tied Ruth with his first swing of the new season. But this event, noteworthy though it may have been, was merely a prelude, and Aaron recognized it as such.

"Seven-fourteen only ties the record," he advised well-wishers at the time. And in yet another ceremony at home plate, he reminded everyone, "It's almost over."

AARON'S INNATE dignity had been jarred in that opening three-game series by the seemingly irresolvable haggling between his employers Bartholomay and manager Eddie Mathews, and Commissioner Kuhn. Bartholomay and Mathews had hoped to keep Aaron out of the lineup for the entire series so that he might entertain the home fans with his immortal swats. When Kuhn suggested forcefully that it was the obligation of every team to put its best lineup on the field at all times and that any violation of this obligation would be regarded by him as sinful, Mathews and Bartholomay relented—but only partially. After Aaron tied the Babe,

Mathews announced that he would bench him for the remaining games of the Reds' series, saving him for the adoring home folks.

This brought an iron rebuke from the commissioner: Aaron would play or Mathews and the Braves must face "serious consequences." This message was delivered after the Braves' second game, in which Aaron did not play. Aaron was in the lineup for 6½ innings the following game, striking out twice and grounding weakly to third in three at bats. The stage— and a stage it seemed—was set for the home opener.

It rained in Atlanta during the day, violently on occasion, but it was warm and cloudy by game time. It began raining again just before Aaron's first inconsequential time at bat, as if Ruth's phantom were up there puncturing the drifting clouds. Brightly colored umbrellas sprouted throughout the ballpark, a brilliant display that seemed to be merely part of the show. The rain had subsided by Aaron's next time up, the air filled now only with tension. Henry wasted little time relieving that tension. It is his way. Throughout his long career Aaron had been faulted for lacking a sense of drama, for failing to rise to critical occasions, as Willie Mays, say, or Ted Williams had. He quietly endured such spurious criticism, then in two memorable games dispelled it for all time. And yet, after it was over, he was Henry Aaron again.

"Right now," he said without a trace of irony, "it feels like just another home run. I felt all along if I got a strike I could hit it out. I just wanted to touch all the bases on this one."

He smiled slightly, conscious perhaps that his words were

not sufficient to the occasion. Then he said what he had been wanting to say since it became apparent that he would eventually pass Ruth and achieve immortality.

"I feel I can relax now. I feel my teammates can relax. I feel I can have a great season."

It is not that he had ever behaved like anyone but Henry Aaron. For this generation of baseball fans and now for generations to come, that will be quite enough.

◇

POSTSCRIPT: *Henry Aaron's ordeal ended at 9:07 p.m. on Monday, April 8—and Ron Fimrite's ordeal, albeit a considerably smaller one, began. The SI associate editor no doubt had been as alarmed as Kuhn had been by Aaron's limited appearances in Cincinnati, which only increased the likelihood that Aaron would make history after Fimrite's Sunday deadline. Indeed, against a tight extended deadline, Fimrite had to scrap his original story—an overview of the chase through No. 714—to account for the record-breaker, which would run as that week's cover story.*

◇

Final Twist of The Drama

BY GEORGE PLIMPTON

At the moment destiny touched Aaron, it reached out
to immortalize a cast of supporting players as well

IT WAS A SIMPLE ACT BY AN UNASSUMING MAN WHICH
touched an enormous circle of people, indeed an entire country. It provided an instant that people would remember for
decades—exactly what they were doing at the time of the
home run that beat Babe Ruth's great record, whether they
were watching it on a television set, or heard it over the car
radio while driving along the turnpike at night, or even
whether a neighbor leaned over a fence and told them about
it the next morning.

For those who sat in the stadium in Atlanta, their recollec-
tions would be more intimate—the sharp cork-popping sound
of the bat hitting the ball, startlingly audible in the split second of suspense before the crowd began a roar that lasted for
more than 10 minutes. Perhaps that is what they would
remember—how people stood in front of their seats and
sucked in air and bellowed it out in a sustained tribute that

few athletes have ever received. Or perhaps they would remember their wonder at how easy and inevitable it seemed—that having opened the season in Cincinnati by hitting the tying home run, No. 714, with his first swing of the year, it was obviously appropriate that the man who has been called "Supe" by his teammates (for Superman) was going to duplicate the feat in Atlanta with his first swing of that game. That was why 53,775 had come. Or perhaps they would remember the odd way the stadium emptied after the excitement of the fourth inning, as if the crowd felt that what they had seen would be diluted by sitting through any more baseball that night.

And then finally there were those few in the core of that immense circle—the participants themselves—who would be the ones most keenly touched: the pitcher, in this case a pleasant, gap-toothed veteran named Al Downing who, of the more than 100 National League pitchers, happened to be the one who threw a fastball at a certain moment that did not tail away properly; the hitter, Henry Aaron himself, for whom the event, despite his grace in dealing with it, had become so traumatic that little in the instant was relished except the relief that it had been done; the Braves announcer, Milo Hamilton, whose imagination for months had been working up words to describe the event to the outside world; and a young bullpen pitcher named Tom House, who would reach up in the air and establish contact with a ball whose value as baseball's greatest talisman had been monetarily pegged at $25,000 and whose sentimental value was incalculable. . . .

THE PITCHER

THE POOR GUY. All those years toiling on the mound, peering down the long alley toward the plate at those constant disturbers of his sense of well-being settling into their stances and flicking their bats—to look down one day and find Henry Aaron there, the large, peaceful, dark face with the big eyes and the high forehead—and knowing that one mistake, one small lapse of concentration and ability would place his name forever in the record books as having thrown the "immortal gopher."

Perhaps there are some pitchers around the league who would not mind being identified with Aaron's eclipsing of Ruth's record. Tracy Stallard, who was a young Boston Red Sox rookie when he gave up the home run to Roger Maris that broke Babe Ruth's record of 60 hit in a year, afterward rather enjoyed the back-of-the-hand notoriety that came with being a victim of Maris's clout, and he would announce, to the point of volunteering, that he was the pitcher responsible. Most pitchers, though, are sensitive enough about their craft to feel differently about such a role. Ray Sadecki once said of Stallard, "I don't want to be him. Everybody knows who he is. Nobody knows *where* he is."

Those scheduled in the rotation against the Atlanta Braves in the final weeks of last season and the opening days of the 1974 schedule were uncomfortably aware they were involved in a sort of cosmic game of Russian roulette, it being inevitable that one of them was going to give up the 715th home run.

The pitcher opposing Aaron in Atlanta on the last day of the 1973 season was Houston Astros lefthander Dave Roberts.

Before the game he sat in front of his locker looking crestfall-
en. "What I should be doing is concentrating on my 17th victory of the year," he said. "But I've been thinking about him. I
thought about him all last night. He was just deposited there
in my mind. What really got me was that I knew he wasn't
thinking about me at all. I wished I'd known his home tele-
phone number, so's I could have called him every 20 minutes—
'How's it going, Hank?'—just to let him know I was around."

In that game Roberts survived three Aaron turns at bat by
giving up three singles that raised the batter's average to .301.
Then, perhaps with his nervous system betraying him, the
pitcher pulled a muscle in his back in the middle of the seventh inning and was removed. In such a situation the relieving pitcher is allowed as much time as he wants to warm up.
Don Wilson, Roberts's reliever, off whom Aaron had hit his
611th home run, said later that as he stood on the mound it
crossed his mind just to keep on warming up indefinitely,
shaking his head and saying, "No, not yet" to the umpire until
the night fell and the moon came up, and perhaps at 10:30 the
next morning some sort of statute of limitations would run
out the season and he would be able to pack up and go home,
sore-armed but assuaged.

The pitcher who through personal experience knows more
about Aaron's specialty than anyone in baseball is the tall,
sidearm, whip-motion Dodgers righthander, Don Drysdale,
now retired from active baseball and working as a broadcaster with the California Angels. Aaron hit the astonishing total
of 17 home runs off him. Next down the line is Claude Osteen,

who has been touched for 13, and when his rotation comes up against the Braves, Drysdale often calls him on the phone (the two were teammates) to remind him that he'd be delighted to be taken off the hook for being Aaron's special patsy ("Now Claude, don't let down. That record is within *reach*").

Drysdale has never felt it was possible to establish much of a "book" on how to pitch to Aaron. "Besides, there never is any set way to pitch to a great hitter," Drysdale says. "If there were, he'd be hitting .220. He's one of those 'five-fingers-and-a-prayer-on-the-ball' hitters. I always used to think that he had a lot of Stan Musial in his stance. From the pitcher's mound they both seem to coil at you. The only sensible thing—if you couldn't get the manager to let you skip a turn against him—was to mix the pitches and keep the ball low, and if you were pitching to spots it was important to miss bad. If you missed good, and the ball got in his power zone, sometimes you were glad it went out of the park and was not banged up the middle."

Drysdale remains in awe of the concussive nature of Aaron's power. He remembers a 250-foot home run Aaron duck-hooked over the short "Chinese Wall" screen in the Los Angeles Coliseum, hit so hard that Drysdale got a crick in his neck from turning abruptly to watch it go by. "It's bad enough to have him hit any home run off you—turning and looking and saying to yourself, 'My God, how far is *that* one going to go.' But with the Coliseum home run. I ended up not only in mental anguish, but literally in physical pain."

At least Drysdale was not around to suffer the wrenching

experience of facing Aaron at this stage in his career. As soon as Aaron was due at the plate the crowd began to stir in anticipation. In the leftfield seats a forest of raised fishnets and gloved hands rose and swayed in expectation. The pitcher was practically the only person in the park who did not want to see the home run hit. Even some of his own teammates would not have been displeased, though they might have been judicious enough to keep it to themselves. In the penultimate week of the 1973 season a scuffle almost broke out in the Los Angeles dugout when a couple of the younger Dodgers, casting aside their team affiliation, carried away in their hope to see a part of history, began urging a long Aaron drive out of the park— "Get on over; get out!" They got some hard stares and shoving from one or two of the more aggressively competitive among their elders, especially Andy Messersmith, who is not only a strong team man but a pitcher hardly agreeable to seeing one of his kind humbled.

The next presentiment that the pitcher had to deal with was the flurry of activity from the umpires as Aaron left the on-deck circle and approached the plate. Since home run No. 710 a ball boy had been rushing out to provide an umpire with a clutch of specially marked balls so that, if the home run were hit, the ball could be positively identified to thwart a horde of people turning up for the $25,000 reward with fakes. Each ball was stamped, last year with an invisible diamond with a number within, this year with two sets of numbers, a marked pattern that lit up under a fluorescent lamp.

All of this could not do much to help the pitcher's

confidence—the scurrying preparations of those attending to an execution. Last year Juan Marichal saw this activity, the plate umpire reaching in a special ball bag at his waist to introduce a special ball to the game, and not being aware of the procedure felt that he was the victim of some odd plot, that perhaps the ball he would get from the umpire was going to pop in two and emit smoke as he gripped it for his screwball. This year it was decided that the base umpire closest to the Braves' dugout would handle the marked balls.

The ball Aaron hit in Cincinnati with his first swing of the season (into a deep enclosure between the outfield fence and the stands known as "the pit") was marked with a pair of 14s and 1s. It was recovered there by a policeman named Clarence Williams, holed up in his canyon with just a piece of sky overhead so that he never saw the home run ball until it came over the fence and bounced at his feet, spattering his uniform with mud. An attendant came rushing down the enclosure toward him, holding open a small paper bag and crying, "Drop it in here! Drop it in here!" And thus it was delivered to Aaron, the ball that tied Ruth's record, shielded as if contaminated from the view of the huge opening-day crowd as the attendant, flanked by two guards, hurried in from centerfield.

Four days later in Atlanta, Al Downing handled two of the prepared balls. The first was marked with 12s and 1s, the 12 arbitrarily picked by Bill Acree, the Braves' equipment manager, and the 1 to show that it was the first of a series of 24 balls specially marked. Downing used it through the first inning when he walked Aaron to massive hoots of derision.

The same ball was tossed to him when Aaron came up again in the fourth. It was thrown out of the game after a pitch in the dirt. From the first-base umpire, Frank Pulli, came a ball marked with a pair of 12s and two 2s.

Downing had realized in the middle of the previous week that he was to pitch the opener in Atlanta. It did not bother him much. Though he is not an overpowering pitcher, he has great confidence. He relies on fine control and a good change of pace. His teammates call him Ace, an encomium for winning 20 games in 1971. He is also called Gentleman Al, for his bearing not only off the field but around the mound where he behaves, according to Vince Scully, the Los Angeles broadcaster, "like a man wearing a bowler hat." Downing is very much his own boss. He shakes off his catcher's signs as many as 25 times a game, relying on his own concepts and on his sense that much of pitching is "feel" ("If you don't feel you can throw a curve at a particular time, there's not much point in trying"). He is such a student of his craft that he has always made it a point to room with a hitter, rare in a society in which there is such a confrontation between the two specialists.

Hank Greenberg, the Detroit home run hitter, always felt that it was essential to detest the fellow opposite. He developed such an antipathy toward pitchers that he would not consider them fellow athletes. They were "throwers." He never thought much of them personally, even those on his own team. Recently he said that the only pitcher on the Tigers he had anything to do with was Fred Hutchinson. "That was because he was a kid under adversity—just coming up—and at the beginning I felt a little sorry for him."

But Downing does not hold to this principle of rancor at all. He says, "It helps a pitcher to be exposed to the enemy camp. For years I roomed with Maury Wills, and it helped my pitching considerably just listening to him talk about hitting. At the very best I knew if I ever had to pitch to him—if either of us was traded away—that I knew something of his thought process as a batter and might be able to take advantage of it.

"Aaron? Well, I'm not sure that rooming with him for 10 years would really help. You can have all the know-how, but if you make one small mistake there's no one in the league who can take advantage of it like he does. He knows what I can throw. He hit two home runs off me last year. But I'm not going to change my pattern. I mustn't go against what I've been successful with.... I shouldn't rearrange pitches that complement each other. If I throw 715 I'm not going to run and hide. There's no disgrace in that. On the other hand, I'm not going to run to the plate to congratulate him. It's a big home run for him, for the game, for the country, but not for me!"

THE HITTER

ON OCCASION, as Henry Aaron sits in the Braves' dugout, he takes off his baseball cap and holds it close against his face. He moves it around until he is able to peer through one of the vent holes in the crown of the cap at the opposing pitcher on the mound. The practice, like focusing through a telescope, serves to isolate the pitcher, setting him apart in a round frame so that Aaron can scrutinize him and decide how he will deal with him once he reaches the plate.

The thought process he goes through during this is deciding what sort of a pitch he will almost surely see, engraving the possibility in his mind's eye so that when the pitch comes (almost as if dictating what he wants) he can truly rip at it. Home run hitters must invariably be guessers of some sort since success at their craft depends on seeing a pitch come down that they expect, so they have time to generate a powerful swing. More than one pitcher has said that Aaron seems to hop on a pitch as if he had called for it. Ron Perranoski, the former Dodgers relief pitcher, once said, "He not only knows what the pitch will be, but where it will be."

Aaron describes his mental preparation as a process of elimination. "Suppose a pitcher has three good pitches: a fastball, a curve and a slider. What I do, after a lot of consideration and analyzing and studying, is to eliminate two of those pitches, since it's impossible against a good pitcher to keep all three possibilities on my mind at the plate. So in getting rid of two, for example, I convince myself that I'm going to get a fastball down low. When it comes, I'm ready. Now, I can have guessed wrong, and if I've set my mind for a fastball it's hard to do much with a curve short of nibbing it out over the infield. But the chances are that I'll eventually get what I'm looking for."

This procedure of "guessing" has many variants. Roger Maris, for example, always went up to the plate prepared to hit a fastball, feeling that he was quick enough to adjust to a different sort of pitch as it flew toward the plate. Most guess hitters play a cat-and-mouse game with the pitcher as the count progresses. What distinguishes Aaron's system is that once he makes up his mind what he will see during a time at bat he never deviates. Aaron has disciplined himself to sit and wait for one sort of pitch, whatever the situation.

One might suppose that a pitcher with a large repertoire of stuff would trouble Aaron—and that indeed turns out to be the case. He shakes his head when he thinks of Marichal. "When he's at the prime of his game he throws a good fastball, a good screwball, a good changeup, a good slider, a good you-have-it . . . and obviously the elimination system can't work; you can't just throw out five or six different pitches in the hope of seeing the one you want; the odds of seeing it would be too much against the batter."

What to do against a Marichal, then? "It's an extra challenge," Aaron says. "I've just got to tune up my bat a little higher. It's a question of confidence, knowing that the pitcher cannot get me out four times without me hitting the ball sharply somewhere."

It is this confrontation between pitcher and hitter that fascinates Aaron, and indeed it is what he likes best about baseball—what he calls "that damn good guessing game."

Obviously there have been the bad times. His manager in the mid-50s, Fred Haney, was thinking of benching him against Drysdale, who was giving him fits in their early matchups. "I had a psychological block going there," Aaron says. "Drysdale was throwing from way out by third base with that sidearm motion of his, and he was mean, and it was hard to hang in there, knowing how mean he was..

"So much of it has to do with concentration. On the day of a night game I begin concentrating at four in the afternoon. Just before I go to bat, from the on-deck circle, I can hear my little girl—she's 12 now—calling from the stands. 'Hey, Daddy! Hey, Daddy!' After the game she says to me, 'Hey, you never look around, Daddy, to wave.' Well, sometimes I look at her, I can't help it, but not too often. I'm looking at the pitcher. I'm thinking very hard about him.

"I started thinking about Al Downing of the Dodgers on the way home from Cincinnati. Basically, I knew what he would like me to hit—his fastball, which tails away and, if he's right, is his best pitch. I knew he didn't want to throw me curveballs, which from a lefthander would come inside, and which I could pull. So I set myself mentally for that one pitch I knew he'd rely on—his fastball. I can discipline myself to wait for that ball. I knew it would come sooner or later. . . . "

There is nothing in Aaron's approach to the plate to suggest such an intensity of purpose. His stride is slow and lackadaisical. (He was called Snowshoes for a time by his teammates for the way he sort of pushes himself along.) He carries his batting helmet on his way to the plate, holding two bats in the other hand. He stares out at the pitcher. He drops the extra bat. Then, just out of the batting box, resting his bat on the ground with the handle end balanced against his thighs, he uses both hands to jostle the helmet correctly into position. He steps into the box. Even here there is no indication of the kinetic possibility, none of the ferocious tamping of his spikes to get a good toe-hold that one remembers of Willie Mays, say, or the quick switching of his bat back and forth as he waits. Aaron steps into the batting box as if he were going to sit down in it somewhere. Downing has said that looking at him during his delivery, he finds it hard to believe Aaron isn't going to take every pitch.

Downing's first pitch to him in the fourth inning was a ball, a changeup that puffed up the dirt in front of the plate. Umpire Dave Davidson turned the ball over, looking at it suspiciously through the bars of his mask and tossed it out. He signaled to umpire Pulli at first base to throw in another of the prepared balls. Downing rubbed it up a bit, then turned and, as the clock on the scoreboard behind him showed 9:07, wheeled and delivered a fastball, aiming low and expecting it to fade away off the outside corner.

The ball rose off Aaron's bat in the normal trajectory of his long hits—the arc of a four-iron shot in golf—ripping out over the infield, the shortstop instinctively bending his knees as if he could leap for it, and it headed for deep left centerfield....

Aaron never saw it clear the fence. Hard as it is to imagine, Aaron says he has never seen one of his home runs land. "That's not what I'm supposed to do," he says. "I've seen guys miss first base looking to see where the ball went. My job is to get down to first base and touch it. Looking at the ball going over the fence isn't going to help. I don't even look at the home runs hit in batting practice. No sense to break a good habit."

So, as he has done countless times, he looked toward first as he ran, dropping his bat neatly just off the base path, and when he saw the exultation of his first-base coach, Jim Busby, he knew for sure that the long chase was over.

THE PITCHER

AL DOWNING did watch the ball go over the fence. He had seen the leftfielder and the centerfielder converge, and he was hoping the wind would hold the ball up. Afterward, when the ceremonies began just off home plate, he went to sit in the Dodgers dugout and looked on.

The delay was of no help to his control, and he was taken out that same inning. He went to the empty Dodgers locker room and dressed. A taxi was ordered for him, and he stood in the stadium tunnel waiting for it. Downing has a very cheery voice that seems to belie the gravity of any situation one might connect him with. "Well, that's that," he said. "I didn't have the rhythm, and the fastball wasn't doing what it was supposed to, which is to drop slightly. I threw a changeup, low, and then I threw a fastball right down the middle. What did I think when he hit it? Damn, there goes our lead. So I went and sat in the dugout. Nobody said anything about the home run. Why should they? We're all grown men. We don't have to console each other. One or two people came by and said, 'We'll get the runs back for you.' "

A photographer appeared with a small souvenir placard handed out by the Braves, testifying that the bearer had been on hand to see the record home run hit. It had a picture of Aaron and the number 715. The photographer wanted

Downing to pose with it, hold it up and smile. Downing shook his head quickly. "I don't think that would prove anything," he said. He looked up and down the tunnel for his taxi.

"I'm more concerned about my next start," he went on. "This thing is over. It's history. It won't bother me. There's only one home run hit off me that's ever stayed in my mind. That was a grand-slam home run that Ken Boyer got in the sixth inning of the 1964 World Series—the one that beat the Yankees 4–3 and turned the whole Series around. I threw him a changeup, and there was a lot of second-guessing that I had thrown him the wrong pitch, that I should have challenged him. I thought about that for a long time. I was 23 at the time. It was a technical consideration. This one? It's more emotional. Well, pitchers don't ever like to give up home runs.

"But," he said in the cheery voice, "I'm not giving myself up to trauma. People will be calling to see if I've jumped out the window yet. I'm not going to wake up in the middle of the night and begin banging on the walls and looking over the sill down into the street. The next time I pitch against him I'll get him out."

A distant roar went up from the crowd. The Braves were having a good inning.

"Your team has made six errors."

"That so? They must be pressing," Downing said. "Everybody's edgy tonight." He craned his neck, looking for his taxi.

THE ANNOUNCER

AT THE SOUND of the ball hitting the bat, in the broadcast booth the chief voice of the Atlanta Braves rose against the tumult to describe the event over the air to his part of the outside world. The voice belonged to Atlanta's local broadcaster, Milo Hamilton, an announcer for the Cubs and the White Sox before coming to the Braves. It was a tremendous moment for him. True, an NBC crew (Curt Gowdy, Tony Kubek and Joe Garagiola) was on hand and so was Scully, the Dodgers announcer for the past 25 years, sending the game back to Los Angeles. Through their combined media, many millions would be made aware of the instant, but none had a more personal involvement than Milo Hamilton. Being with the Braves, he was the only broadcaster in the country who had known for months that at some point he would be describing Aaron's historic home run. His situation was extraordinary for a sportscaster. While he had to verbalize instantly into a microphone what he saw, in the case of Aaron's home run, since it was inevitable, Hamilton had an opportunity to prepare a sentence so perfect that if it worked, if enough people heard it and commented on it, it had an excellent chance to slip into *Bartlett's Familiar Quotations* alongside "One small step. . . ."

It was a unique situation. Almost invariably, a momentous comment in sports reporting is made spontaneously, under pressure and against the crowd noise, so that a common characteristic is often that the key sentences are repeated. There was a flurry of repetitions when Russ Hodges, ordinarily a somewhat phlegmatic sportscaster, gave his on-the-spot report of Bobby Thomson's "miracle of Coogan's Bluff" home run in the Dodgers-Giants playoff game in 1951. "The Giants win the pennant! The Giants win the pennant! The Giants win the pennant! The Giants win the pennant ... I don't believe it! I don't believe it! I DO NOT BELIEVE IT!"

Describing the extraordinary home run of Ted Williams in his last time at bat in the majors, Curt Gowdy had a brace of repeated sentences: "It's got a chance! It's got a chance! And it's gone!. . ." All of this, in fact, in somewhat restrained fashion, since in an earlier inning Williams had hit a long fly ball that Gowdy described as if it were going into the seats. He did not want to be fooled again.

Phil Rizzuto, the Yankee broadcaster, had a quasi-opportunity, much like Hamilton's, to prepare for Roger Maris's 61st home run, which was a strong possibility though hit on the last day of the 1961 season. Obviously, he did not do so, since his radio commentary, utilizing his favorite epithet, was absolutely predictable. "Holy Cow!" he cried. "That's gonna be it."

Sportscasters all take a dim view of preparing material in advance, feeling that spontaneity must be the key essential of their craft, the thing that so often produces the most noteworthy effect. Red Barber remembers that when he was broadcasting the famous Cookie Lavagetto double that destroyed the no-hitter of the Yankees' Bill Bevens in the 1947 World Series, he described the high drive and how it hit the fence, and here came the tying run and now the winning run, and here was Lavagetto being mobbed by his own teammates, and near beaten up, and then Barber gave a sigh, worn-out by all the drama, and he said memorably, "Well, I'll be a suck-egg mule."

Telecasting, obviously, gives the announcer a better chance to drop in a bon mot, since the picture on the set, if the technicians are on their toes, portrays so much. Barber was the television commentator the day Maris broke Ruth's record, and he started out, "It's a high fly ball. . . ." and he paused, noting in the TV monitor that the flight of the ball was clearly shown, and then remembering that a Sacramento restaurateur had offered a large sum of money for the ball, he announced when it dropped into the stands, "It's 61 and $5,000!"

Hamilton would agree with Barber and the others about spontaneity. "It's very much my cup of tea," he says. But on his speaking tours this past winter he realized that so much curiosity was being generated by what he was going to say at the climactic moment that he felt bound to work something up. In the evenings he would sit around and let his imagination take over: as he watched the Aaron home run arch into the seats his lips murmured; the sentences formed; the facts crowded his mind, especially the similarities between Aaron and Babe Ruth—that both were born just a day apart in February, both hitting the 714th home run at the same age (40) and both as members of the Braves organization. Hamilton decided to announce much of this material as Aaron circled the bases after hitting 715, using each base as marker along the way (". . . he steps on *second* . . . and the Babe's great record, nearly two-score years old . . . and he steps on *third* . . . a great day for Aquarians! Both Henry and the Babe. . . . ").

As for the phrases at the moment of impact, Hamilton decided on "Henry has tied the Babe!" for home run 714, and for 715, the tie breaker, he chose, after much thought. "Baseball has a new home run king! It's Henry Aaron!"—not earth-shaking (nor in the case of the latter especially grammatical), but functional. Hamilton realized that anything more ornate would sound hollow and forced.

When the great moment came, however, spontaneity took over despite Hamilton's best intentions. The planned sequence of comparing Ruth and Aaron was wiped out of mind because of the speed with which Aaron circled the bases, not being one to slow down and glory in the occasion, the tremendous crowd noise and a violent eruption of fireworks exploding above the centerfield rim of the stadium. Even the word "king," which he had intended to say, came out "champion." "It's gone!" he cried. "It's 715! There's a new home run champion of all time! And it's Henry Aaron!" But mainly, Hamilton was startled during his commentary by something he had never seen before in his nine years of describing the Braves in action: as Aaron turned third base, his solemn face suddenly broke into a bright grin, as surprising to see considering his usual mien as if he had started doing an Irish jig coming down the base path toward the plate. Hamilton was struck by it, but he never had time to describe it to his audience; by the time he recovered, Aaron was running into the pack of players and dignitaries, with more streaming from both benches and the grandstand, and he had these things to describe to his listeners. But Aaron beaming was the one sight, he said later, that while it had never found its way into his commentary he would particularly remember of that day. . . .

THE HITTER

AARON HIMSELF does not remember smiling, or very much else about that run around the bases. The tension, the long haul, the discomfiture of the constant yammering, the hate mail—perhaps all of that was symbolized by 715, and to hit it produced a welcome mental block. Aaron has always said that the most important home run in his life was 109, an undistinguished number, but it was a home run hit in the 11th inning of a 2–2 tie game that defeated the St. Louis Cardinals and gave the Braves the 1957 pennant. Aaron has a very clear memory of his reaction as he circled the base paths in that enormous tumult of rejoicing. He suddenly remembered Bobby Thomson's Miracle Home Run and how he had heard about it over somebody's radio as he was coming home from school in Mobile and how he had begun running as if coming down from third toward his teammates waiting at an imaginary plate. "That had always been my idea of the most important homer," Aaron said after hitting his pennant-winner. "Now I've got one for myself. For the first time in my life, I'm excited." A home run of that sort, meaning one that produced a playoff or championship victory, is obviously his idea of an "important" home run.

But about 715 he remembers only his relief that it was over with and the vague happiness; that his legs seemed rubbery as he took the tour of the bases, the Dodgers second baseman and shortstop sticking out their hands to congratulate him. "I don't remember the noise," he said, trying to recall, "or the two kids that I'm told ran the bases with me. My teammates at home plate, I remember seeing them. I remember my mother out there, and she hugging me. That's what I'll remember more than anything about that home run when I think back on it. I don't know where she came from, but she was there. . . ."

THE RETRIEVER

THERE WAS hardly a fan who turned up in the leftfield seats for the Atlanta opener who did not firmly believe that he was going to catch the Aaron home run. Many of them brought baseball gloves. A young Atlantan from the highway department had established himself in the front row, wielding a 15-foot-long bamboo pole with a fishnet attached. He was proficient with it, sweeping it back and forth over the Braves bullpen (at home his stepsister threw up baseballs over the winter for him to practice on), though the closest he had come to catching anything with his gear had been a batting-practice home run hit into the bullpen enclosure the year before by a catcher named Freddie Velazquez. He missed sweeping it in by a couple of feet.

The leftfield stands of Atlanta Stadium contain the cheapest seats in the ballpark and perhaps its most knowledgeable and intractable fans. They have a close affinity with Aaron. He stands immediately in front of them when the Braves are in the field, and they look down at the big blue 44 on the back of his uniform and watch the way he rests his oversized glove ("These days I need all the glove I can get") on his hip between pitches. They rise and cheer him when he walks out to his position, and as they do he lifts his throwing hand in an awkward, shy gesture to acknowledge them.

The Braves' outfield is bordered by a six-foot-high wire-mesh fence that runs around the perimeter of the grass. In the space between it and the high wall of the stands are the two bullpens. The visitors' bullpen is in the rightfield corner. The Braves' mascot, Chief Noc-A-Homa, sits in his tepee on the leftfield foul line, adjacent to the Atlanta bullpen, and when a Braves batter hits a home run he steps out in his regalia and does a war dance. The Braves' bullpen being immediately under the leftfield wall, the fans with front-row seats can look down and see the catchers resting their right knees on towels to keep their pants legs from getting dusty as they warm up the relief pitchers.

The Atlanta pitching staff was the weakest in the National League last year (one reason why the Braves, despite a Murderer's Row of Aaron, Darrell Evans, Dusty Baker, Mike Lum and Dave Johnson, who last year broke Rogers Hornsby's home run record for second basemen, were not pennant contenders), and the leftfield fans have the same sort of despairing affection for the relievers that Mets fans had for their team in its early, bleak days. "We *know* the pitchers out here," one Atlanta fan said. "In the expensive part of the stadium they never see them long enough to get acquainted.

They go in and they're bombed and they're on their way to the showers, which are kept going full and heavy. They never turn off the showers once the starting pitcher is knocked out."

The main reason for sitting in the leftfield corner, of course, is that the majority of Aaron's home runs are pulled toward there, either to land in the stands or in the enclosure where a denizen of the bullpen or Chief Noc-A-Homa can retrieve them. Noc-A-Homa has seen every home run Aaron has hit in Atlanta Stadium since 1969, with the exception of No. 698, which he missed because he was trying to find a chair for one of the bullpen pitchers. He has not retrieved an Aaron home run since '72, being too busy doing his celebratory foot-stomping dance. But, brisk of foot himself and outfitted with a lacrosse stick for additional reach, he had seen himself as a possible retriever should 715 drop in the enclosure. When Aaron really tags one, the homer flies over the enclosure and drops in the general-admission areas, where a pyramid of struggling people immediately forms over the ball.

Last year a man named A.W. Kirby from Old Hickory, Tenn. sprinted down an aisle, dived over a chair and, after suffering a broken fingernail and lacerated wrists and ankles in a tremendous scuffle, came up with home run 693, coincidentally the second of those Aaron hit off Al Downing in 1973. Mr. Kirby thought the ball was worth $1,700. His son had misinformed him.

The abrasions and thumps suffered in the pileup over 715 would be worth it. A high of $25,000 (by both Sammy Davis Jr. and an anonymous Venezuelan fan) had been offered for the ball. The retriever would be photographed giving it back to Aaron, and his face would shine out of the country's sports pages, and even if on the periphery, he would know something of the excitement of being touched by the moment.

Eventually the prize would go to the Hall of Fame at Cooperstown, N.Y., to join other great talismans of baseball history under their domes of glass—among them, Roger Maris' 61st and Babe Ruth's 714th and last home run, each with the name of the retriever included.

There are several astonishing things about Ruth's last home run, the first being that it was even recovered at all. It was the third he hit that day (May 25, 1935), and it was the first hit out of Pittsburgh's Forbes Field since its construction in 1909, an accomplishment that lasted until 1950, when Ted Beard, a Pirate outfielder, was the first of a select group (including Willie Stargell, who has done it a number of times) to join him.

The Pirate pitcher on the mound that day against Ruth and the Boston Braves was Guy Bush, who had come in to relieve the starter, Red Lucas, off whom the Babe had hit the first of his trio. Bush, who now lives on a farm in Mississippi, remembers that the "book" on Ruth (he refers to the Bambino as the Big Bamboo) was to throw him a slow curve. "Well, sir, I threw the slow curve, and he hit this little Chinese home run down the rightfield line—which was no distance at all—20 feet back into the stands for his second of the day. That made me so mad that when he came up again at the back end of the game I called Tommy Padden, my catcher, out to the mound, and I said, 'Tommy, I don't think the Big Bamboo can hit my fastball.' I *didn't* think so, sir. He had a stance at the plate where he near had his back to the pitcher; he was so far turned around that I could see the number 3 on his uniform: I didn't think the monkey could come around quick enough on my fastball to get his bat on it. So I told Tommy that I was going to challenge him with the fastball. In fact, I told Tommy to go back and *tell* the Big Bamboo what I was going to do— that I was going to *damn* him to hit my fastball. That's how confident I was. Now Tommy Padden has passed away, poor soul, and I can't tell you for sure whether he told the Bamboo what I was going to do. But I can tell you this, sir, that I threw two fastballs, and he hit the second one for the longest ball I ever saw—it cleared those whole three decks—and I was too surprised to be mad anymore."

The ball Ruth hit sailed over the heads of a group of boys who happened to be standing at the corner of Bouquet and Joncire and bounced into a construction lot, where it was retrieved by a youngster named Henry (Wiggy) Diorio. He took it around to the Schenley Hotel, where the Braves were staying, for Ruth's autograph. At that time no one, much less the Babe (who decided to retire a few games later), knew that the ball would be the last he would ever hit out of a ballpark. He autographed the ball for young Wiggy and said that as far as he was concerned it was just another home run. As for Roger Maris' home run, that was caught by a young truck driver named Sal Durante. He saw the ball begin its rise, and he hopped up on his seat (No. 4 in Box 163 D in Section 33 at

Yankee Stadium) and made a one-handed grab. He shouted, "I got it! I got it!" and was immediately engulfed by a tide of fans trying to wrest the ball away. The ball was worth $5,000 to him—a pleasant windfall for Durante (who was going to present the ball to Maris anyway) and made his stadium seat, according to *The New York Times* the next day, the most "profitable in baseball history."

In Atlanta most of the home runs do not reach the stands but fall in the enclosure. There, the Braves themselves had decided that if any member of the bullpen caught the ball, it should be delivered immediately to Aaron. Coach Ken Silvestri was asked to supervise the procedure. When Aaron came up he spotted his bullpen crew along the wall, about five yards apart. In the fourth inning Silvestri stationed himself close to the leftfield line in the hope Aaron would pull the ball sharply. He looked around for his big flexible mitt used to catch knuckleballs and discovered that Gary Gentry, a *pitcher* what's more, had swiped it, leaving Silvestri with a regular catcher's glove, which is not the best piece of equipment to catch a long drive. He was just about to call across and cuss out Gentry when Downing began his windup and threw. . . .

The last man in the line toward centerfield was lefthander Tommy House, one of the staff's short relievers. He is called Puma by his teammates for the way he bounces around during the pepper games and thumps down catlike on the ball, a young Southern Cal graduate in awe of what happened.

"The whole thing blew my mind. The ball came right at me, just rising off the bat on a line. If I'd frozen still like a dummy, the ball would have hit me right in the middle of the forehead. Drop the ball? No way. It never occurred to me; it wouldn't to anyone who's been catching fly balls since he was a kid. The only vague problem was someone directly above me who had a fishnet on a pole; he couldn't get it operating in time. I've been getting a lot of kidding, particularly from the other people out in the bullpen, because I've got my masters degree in marketing and I don't suppose my professors would give me high marks for opportunism, with so much being offered for the ball.

"But I'm not at all sorry. What made it worthwhile was what I saw when I ran in with the ball, holding it in my gloved hand, running really fast—in fact my teammates joked afterward that it was the fastest I'd run in a couple of years—really just wanting to get rid of it, to put it in Henry's hand. In that great crowd around home plate I found him looking over his mother's shoulder, hugging her to him, and suddenly I saw what many people have never been able to see in him—deep emotion. I'd never seen that before. He has such cool. He never gets excited. He's so stable. And I looked, and he had tears hanging on his lids. I could hardly believe it. 'Hammer, here it is,' I said. I put the ball in his hand. He said 'Thanks, kid,' and touched me on the shoulder. I kept staring at him. And it was then that it was brought home to me what this home run meant, not only to him, but to all of us. . . ."

Aaron's most significant home runs have been marked where they came down—No. 500 by a white square on the Fan-A-Gram electric announcement board, No. 600 by the appropriate numerals painted in white high on the wall down the leftfield foul line and No. 700 by a seat painted red amongst its baby-blue fellows in the leftfield stands. The Braves management has not decided what to do about commemorating the spot where No. 715 came down. A plaque had been thought of for placement in the wall or in the stands, but no one was prepared for House's catch. Some clubhouse wags have suggested that a replica of the pitcher, life-size, should be set out there, if not the original article, stuffed, a gloved arm outstretched.

A more eloquent testimonial than anything the Braves management can probably think up is already in place just across the expressway from the stadium—a life-size concrete statue of Aaron set up in the cluttered front yard of a 70-year-old black gravestone cutter named E. M. Bailey. Bailey works only in concrete (marble is far too expensive for his customers), and each of his headstones, with the name and date chiseled on it, sells for $10. In his off time he works on pieces of sculpture— massive-winged birds with thin, curved necks, a pair of girls bent like mangrove roots in a wild dance, a memorial to John F. Kennedy with *Air Force One* flying above the White House— all his constructions made of Portland cement.

He began working on the Aaron sculpture last spring and had it finished and brightly painted (Aaron's uniform in appropriate blue, white and red) just in time to move it, with the assistance of three helpers, into his small front yard on the night of the opener. The statue weighs more than 2,000 pounds. It shows Aaron at the completion of the swing of a massive bat, his eyes, somewhat slanted in Oriental style, watching the ball sail off on its flight. When it was in place, the children came down the street, leaning up against a chicken-wire fence to look up briefly at the statue on their way home to watch the game on TV.

Bailey, somewhat exhausted by his afternoon's labors with the statue, relaxed in his springback chair for the game. His wife sat across the room. When Aaron hit No. 715 the two could hear the shouts rising along the street from the neighbors' houses. "Just then," Bailey says, "I kind of thought back, and when I realized how far he had come and what the hardships were and what it means when one of us makes good, well, I shed a little tear over that, setting there in my chair. My wife never knew. Oh my, no! I never let on. She never saw."

◇

POSTSCRIPT: *It was widely assumed that the 1974 season would be Aaron's last as a ballplayer. The Braves, in fact, held a day in his honor in July and the rest of baseball followed suit, turning the season's final months into a farewell tour. Aaron's last days as a Braves player, however, were tinged with bitterness. The front office showed little interest in keeping him around in anything more than a low-level capacity and only 11,000 fans showed up for his final home game. "There was no real warmth between the city and me," Aaron wrote in his autobiography, "and it was time for us to go our separate ways." His playing days in Atlanta might have been over, but there was one city eager to receive him.*

◇

POST 715

◇

Men with a Yen
For the Fences

BY DICK YOUNG

*It was Mr. A over Mr. Oh in an international
home run derby between two world-famous sluggers*

AGAINST THE IMPROBABLE BACKGROUND OF NEW YORK
Mets wives chanting, "Let's go, Hank," Henry Aaron swung
his mighty Ed Kranepool bat at a very fat batting-practice
pitch and sent it soaring into the leftfield bleachers of Tokyo's
Korakuen Stadium. Thus did Bad Henry complete a short
day's work for $50,000 last week. He turned away with a
pleased smile and walked off a baseball field wearing, for perhaps the last time, the Braves' uniform that he has fitted so
nobly these past 21 years.

When next you see Henry Aaron swing a bat, it will be for
the strange Milwaukee Brewers, in the strange American
League, but in not-so-strange Milwaukee County Stadium.
It was there, in 1954, that a lean 20-year-old kid from
Alabama broke into the major leagues with a franchise
called the Milwaukee Braves, originally from Boston and
destined for Atlanta. In the course of the next two decades

Henry Aaron was to hit 733 home runs and announce his retirement as an active player, effective at the end of the 1974 season.

"I had no intention of playing again," he said in Tokyo, fondling a bat in the confining clubhouse built for smaller ballplayers. "I'm sincere about that. I intended to move into the front office of the Braves. I was wrong. Life changes."

One of life's little changes had brought him to Japan for a home run hitting contest of international proportions. Sadaharu Oh, the Babe Ruth of Japan, would cross bats with Aaron, the Babe Ruth of America.

This momentous challenge had been arranged, not through the state departments of the United States and Japan, not through the offices of American Baseball Commissioner Bowie Kuhn and Japanese Baseball Commissioner Nobumoto Ohama, but through a much stronger force, CBS Television. Frank Chirkinian, executive producer of the network, offered $50,000 to Aaron, six million yen ($20,000) to Oh and a silver bowl to the winner.

CONVENIENTLY, THE Mets were in Japan for an 18-game goodwill tour—goodwill deriving from their winning just one of the first six games. The home run contest would be taped as a preliminary event to a Nov. 2 game between the Mets and a Japanese All-Star team, for showing later that day on CBS.

The principals had their pregame meeting in a special room in Korakuen Stadium. You could tell it was a special room, because on the door were the words SPECIAL ROOM. Inside, Frank Chirkinian was briefing Hank Aaron.

"We'll open with you wishing him good luck," Chirkinian said to Henry. Then, to anybody, "How do you say good luck?"

"*Gom-bah-tay,*" somebody said.

"*Hai, gambatte,*" said Sadaharu Oh, smiling broadly.

Chirkinian kidded Aaron: "You think you can do that without a cue card?"

"*Gom-bah-tay,*" said Aaron, confidently.

Aaron was cool. Just how significant he considered the contest could be deduced from the fact that he had brought no bats across the Pacific with him. In the morning he had taken 10 minutes of preliminary batting practice, using two of Oh's bats and cracking one. Then he borrowed one of Kranepool's 220-A Adirondack Bat Company models. It is an ounce lighter and half an inch longer than Aaron's 34-ounce, 35-inch personalized bat, but "the handle feels good," said Henry. To a ballplayer, grip comfort is important.

The next item was the selection of pitchers. Met coaches Rube Walker and Joe Pignatano split the warmup pitching to Aaron, and Henry decided that Pignatano's delivery, which was more overhanded, was better suited to the background. Mr. Oh, a lefty hitter, loyally stayed with Kiniyasu Mine, the regular righthanded batting-practice pitcher for the Yomiuri Giants.

In his 16 seasons with the Giants, Oh has hit 634 home runs. Oh is 34, a full six years younger than Aaron, and has said that he intends to play six more seasons. He has been averaging well over 40 home runs a year. It does not take a computer to figure that by 1980 he could soar past Aaron's ultimate total. What then? Is the world then to recognize Sadaharu Oh as the greatest home run hitter who ever lived? Would Henry Aaron then be willing to concede the point?

"That would be totally unfounded," said Aaron, when asked the hypothetical question. "I don't think there's any comparison with the home runs he hits here and the ones I hit in the States."

The ballparks in Japan are smaller, the fences shorter. At Korakuen Stadium, the big one, it is 90 meters down each line, or 292.5 feet. On the other hand, the regular season is only 130 games, compared to 162 in the States. Additionally, Oh is walked 150 to 160 times a year, mostly intentionally, so he has about half as many at bats as Aaron, who has drawn more than 80 walks in a season only twice in his career.

IF ALL THIS sounds reminiscent of the Aaron-Ruth controversy that raged around Henry's assault on the Babe's total, that's not half of the irony. Sadaharu Oh's father came from China. (Chinese were brought to Japan a generation ago to do the menial work.) Socially, it has been an ordeal for Oh to establish his greatness. It must amuse Henry Aaron when he recalls the reluctance of Ruthophiles to accept a black man as the new home run king.

Sadaharu Oh is the reincarnation of Mel Ott with high

cheekbones. He cocks his front leg in an exaggerated lift as the pitcher releases the ball. He is not big (5' 10", 174 pounds) but he is powerful, and he has a magnificently fluid home run stroke. He won the toss and was first up. The format had been agreed upon: Each man would hit 20 fair balls, alternating in five-swing segments.

Oh drove three of his first five balls high and far into the seats in right, and some 50,000 fans cheered, and some 50,000 cameras clicked.

Now it was Henry's turn. The stadium grew respectfully quiet. Aaron drove Pignatano's first serve deep into the left-field bleachers. "Ho, ho," ho-hoed Mets' ace Tom Seaver, clearly delighted. The fans ooooohed respectfully. Next came a single, then a second homer, a line drive, another single, a pop-up. At the end of the first round, Sadaharu Oh led 3–2.

Now there was doubt among the Mets, and among the Mets wives, seated in a chauvinistic bloc behind the dugout. Could Henry lose? After all, he was out of shape. It had been a month since his season ended. Oh had been playing right along. He was keyed. He had timing. Timing is everything in hitting.

In the second round, Oh blasted three more homers, one of them booming off the back wall, 30 rows beyond the fence. It was 6–2 as Henry came up for his second five swings. Five drives later it was 6–6. With a championship burst, Aaron had boomed four homers and just missed a fifth, a drive that bounced on one hop against the fence.

The tide swung to Aaron in the third round. Oh, seemingly feeling the pressure, hit only one homer, on his first swing. Then the bat grew heavy in his hands and he topped four straight pitches. There was a rumbling of discontent in the stands.

"The gamblers are getting nervous up there," said Jack Aker to Seaver. "A lot of yen are riding on this."

Aaron tied it 7–7 with his second swing, moved ahead 8–7 with a cheapie that tantalizingly dropped into the first row, then boomed one halfway up the bleachers to take command, 9–7, with five shots left to each man.

Then came the inevitable controversy. Oh's first swing in the final segment sent a liner into the first row, making it 9–8. His next was a towering fly down the right line. It came down, quite clearly, some five, six feet foul.

"Fair ball," said the motion of the Japanese umpire in the right corner.

"Foul ball," motioned Chris Pelekoudas, the National League ump working the plate. A tentative run was flashed on the electric scoreboard in center.

"Mr. Oh," said Pelekoudas respectfully, "that ball was foul."

"Yes, it was foul," said Sadaharu Oh, who speaks some English and is fluent in class. Whereupon Pelekoudas, waving both of his hands vehemently overhead, signaled foul ball. The scoreboard reverted to 9–8, and the action resumed.

Oh was to hit one more homer in his remaining tries, bring-

ing up Aaron with the score 9–9 and five shots at getting one
home run to win.

"Let's go, Hank," screeched the Mets' female auxiliary.

"I never thought I'd hear my wife pulling for Henry," said
Jerry Koosman. Aaron drove one deep to left, just short of
the fence. The next was a groundout to short. Then came a
beauty, a mighty drive, far enough, obviously, but close to
the line.

"Stay fair," said a Met. It did, and Aaron turned, smiling,
satisfied, and walked away. The fans applauded respectfully.
Reluctantly. Damn Yankees. Don't they ever lose?

IN THE clubhouse Henry Aaron looked ahead. "It should be
settled soon," he said. "My attorney is talking with the
Brewers today, I think. I hear that the Braves have asked for
Dave May for me and are getting him.

"Like I told you, I made my statement about retiring
because I was thinking I'd be with the Braves for the rest of
my life."

He shrugged. "I found out what I guess I should have
known all along," he said. "There's no sentiment. It's all business. You better believe it."

Within hours the deal with the Brewers' was closed—
Aaron for May and a minor leaguer to be named later.
Obviously the Braves had made Aaron a front-office propo-
sition far short of his expectations. Now, it is believed, he
will become the general manager of the Brewers, or be
entrusted with some similarly high-level position, after he

plays for them one year. He is purchasing the job from owner Bud Selig with one more season of sweat and aching 41-year-old muscle.

Aaron went back to the Hotel Okura and rested. He looked at his newest trophy, and something caught his eye. His name was misspelled. *Arron*, it read.

$$\diamondsuit$$

POSTSCRIPT: *The Brewers, in fact, were banking on a few more years of sweat and aching muscle from Aaron, who would sign a two-year deal for nearly half a million dollars. Meanwhile, Oh would play six more seasons for Yomiuri and finish his pro career with 868 home runs, creating a small dispute about whom the true home run king was. That never came between Mr. A and Mr. Oh, who would team up in several business and charitable ventures.*

9:07 p.m., April 8, 1974: "It's 715! There's a new home run champion of all time!"

A rubber-legged Aaron recalled seeing his teammates and mom at home plate ...

... but had no recollection of the two fans who swarmed him between second and third.

"I just thank God that it's all over," Aaron said of No. 715.

After he retired, Aaron confessed to fears that an assassin might have been in the crowd.

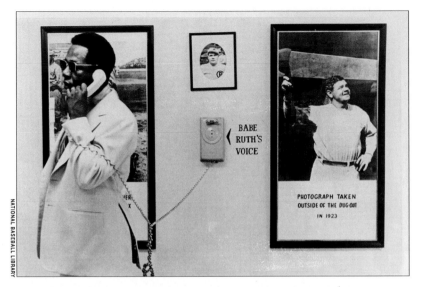

BABE RUTH'S VOICE

PHOTOGRAPH TAKEN OUTSIDE OF THE DUG-OUT IN 1923

In 1982 the Hammer received the call to join the Babe in Cooperstown.

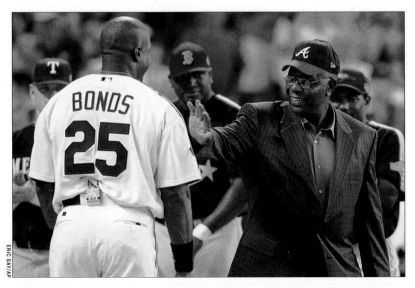

BONDS 25

When they met at the '04 All-Star Game, Bonds was 74 homers behind Aaron.

In 1999 President Clinton was on hand to celebrate Aaron's 65th birthday.

From left: Hall of Famers Aaron, Ryne Sandberg, Lou Brock, Phil Niekro and Robin Roberts at a 2005 Senate hearing on drug testing.

In his Atlanta attic Aaron preserved the hate mail from the summer of the chase.

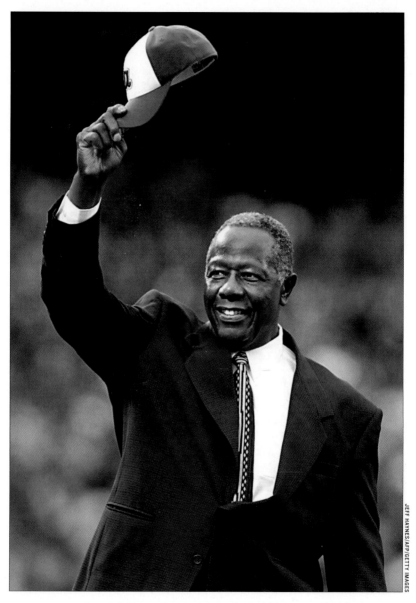

Aaron was honored before Game 4 of the '02 Angels-Giants World Series.

◇

Back Where
He Belongs

BY LARRY KEITH

Milwaukee's finest slugger returned, somewhat unexpectedly,
to the site of many of his greatest triumphs

IF THE RELATIONSHIP BETWEEN HENRY AARON AND THE
baseball fans of Milwaukee is "one of the great love affairs of
all time," as someone has said, then his return to County
Stadium last week as a Milwaukee Brewer was one of the
grand reunions.

A club record turnout of 48,160 showed its hankering for
Hank by waving pennants and serenading him with a ditty to
the tune of *Hello, Dolly.*

Welcome home, Henry.
Welcome home, Henry.
It's so nice to have you back
Where you belong.

The game itself, a 6–2 defeat of the Cleveland Indians,
showed Aaron to be looking swell and going strong. He did

not blast a home run, but he did get his first American League hit, run and RBI.

Anticipation for the day had been building since early November, when Aaron received a 3 a.m. phone call in Japan announcing the termination of his 21-year career with the Braves of Milwaukee and Atlanta. "I'm going home," he told the caller, Brewers' president Bud Selig. "Isn't that great?"

For Aaron, home is where the heart is. He was born in Mobile more than four decades ago and spent the last nine years in Atlanta. But Milwaukee is where he got his major league start, enjoyed 12 of his best seasons and hit more than half of his record 733 home runs. When the Braves did not offer him the player-development job he wanted for this season, he followed Babe Ruth's precedent of 40 years ago and returned to the city where it all began. The American League's designated-hitter rule will keep Aaron busy the next two years. After that he can work with young prospects "to perpetuity," as Selig puts it. "There's nothing I'm more proud of than bringing Henry Aaron back to Milwaukee," Selig says. "And that includes giving this town a new franchise five years ago."

The day before the Brewers' home opener, Aaron returned the compliment at a civic luncheon. "I always thought you people were responsible for my career," he said. "When I made mistakes on the field, you stuck with me. Young players are blessed to be in a city like this."

It was clear and cold on Aaron's homecoming day, and

when he arrived at the stadium an autograph seeker stopped him to say, "I haven't been back here since you left."

Once inside the clubhouse Aaron went to his cubicle, where he smoked a cigarette, drank a cup of coffee, sang a snatch of song: "He's got the whole world in His hands."

Among the other ballplayers getting dressed was the Brewers' shortstop, Robin Yount. At 19 he is the youngest player in the majors. Aaron, the oldest, batted .314 the year Yount was born.

"At first I didn't know how to address him," said Yount. "I was kind of scared, but finally I went up to him and said something like, 'Hello, Mr. Aaron.' "

Surveying his new-old surroundings before the game, the 41-year-old Aaron said, "There isn't a player on this team who was around the year we won the World Series. But this is a good young team. I just want to help them win. I'll be able to play more this year, maybe 150 games. I could hit 30 to 35 home runs if I do. With that bat I'm as young as anybody."

Aaron is not as young as he was, however. In 17 spring training games he batted .226 and, during the season's first two games in Boston, he was the only regular to go hitless. "It takes me longer to get prepared," he said. "I know what I can do. In Boston all I saw was slow stuff. I like the high strike zone the American League has, but I don't think the pitchers throw as hard."

On the field the press pressed in. Yes, said Aaron yet again, he was glad to be back. Yes, Milwaukee is a great town. After the crowd had sung its welcome he walked out of the dugout to a standing ovation that lasted almost two minutes. "It was a great feeling, a great feeling," he said later. "Something I'll always remember." From home plate he told the crowd, "I've always felt a special place in my heart for Milwaukee. I hope we can write a new chapter in the hearts of so many wonderful fans."

Nice, but not the kind of drama his bat has provided so often in the past. That opportunity came with his turn at bat in the first inning. Indians pitcher Jim Perry kept his sliders low, however, and Aaron could do no better than walk.

Two innings later he came up again, with nobody out and men on first and third. He asked manager Del Crandall if he should try a sacrifice bunt, but Crandall told him to swing away. He did, hitting a ground ball to short which forced the runner at second but allowed the man on third to score. Moments later Aaron was retired himself, when Crandall ordered a steal that was as unsuccessful as it was unexpected. (Aaron, who had once consistently reached double digits in stolen bases, had attempted all of nine swipes in his final four seasons in Atlanta.)

Before batting in the sixth inning, Aaron went into the clubhouse to warm up, returning in time to see John Briggs lead off with a home run. Then he stirred the crowd with a long foul before ripping a line drive hit off third baseman Buddy Bell's glove. The crowd roared—as if, Aaron noted later, "I'd hit a grand slam."

He grounded out in the seventh, finishing one for three. "I

felt good," he concluded, "the best I've felt yet. I just hope all the excitement is over now so I can play baseball."

For Henry Aaron, the player who made Milwaukee famous, that will take a while.

◇

POSTSCRIPT: *In his two seasons in Milwaukee, Aaron hit 22 home runs, the 755th and final of which came off the Angels' Dick Drago on July 20, 1976. In addition to the home run record, Aaron finished his 23-year career with major league marks for hits by a righthanded hitter (3,771) and RBIs (2,297). He tied the Babe for most runs scored (2,175). After singling on the final weekend of the '76 season against the Tigers, Aaron recalled thinking, "I didn't care very much about breaking another tie with Ruth. I sort of liked the idea of sharing something with the Babe."*

◇

A Prisoner
Of Memory

BY MIKE CAPUZZO

*Eighteen years after he broke the Babe's record, the
reigning Home Run King was still haunted by the past*

TO FIND THE HOME RUN KING IN THE 19TH YEAR OF HIS
reign, you must journey south from Atlanta, across pine country, to a far and high wall, as if you were seeking an exiled ruler
in an old and sad story. The Home Run King prefers to be
alone, trusts few strangers to enter his vast, secluded estate.

You arrive at a 10-foot-high iron fence that sweeps across
the horizon, bare and stark and tipped with steel points. This
is the fence that Henry Aaron built after he hit 714 and 715
and tried to put them out of his mind forever.

A sensor detects your car as you drive between massive brick
pillars and down the entrance road to a double gate. It is locked.
To your left is a shiny steel security box. A human voice, familiar but horribly altered, inquires of your business. In the stillness you find yourself shouting an answer. There are two shrill
electronic beeps, the grinding motor of gates opening. . . .

Up a hill and around a bend, the Home Run King stands in

front of his redbrick Georgian mansion holding the security remote control, his face hard and shut like a door. Henry Aaron nods, unsmiling, and as you get closer, you notice that he's looking far over your shoulder. It's an old habit he picked up 19 years ago, in the summer of "the Chase." *Never waste eye contact on the fellow in front of you.* That summer, he never knew for sure who was coming at him, or from where. Never knew if he could just grin and give an autograph. Never knew if his bodyguard might have to punch a menacing fan or even pull out his .38.

Quietly, Aaron leads you to his family room, sits on a sofa, offers you a drink. He is 58 now, 20 pounds over his playing weight, graying. But the forearms under the silk print shirt are still wide and hard, the wrists still like the oak handles of hammers. The family room has 22 picture windows, affording distant views of sun-dappled woods, a tennis court, a five-acre pond stocked with bass. This is one of the few places on earth where the Home Run King is comfortable.

"I never finish a drink anywhere, even a glass of water," Aaron is saying, "unless I'm right here at home." In a bar or other public place, he explains, "you'll never find me going back to a drink after I've been to the men's room." He never knows, he says, when someone might try to drug him, poison him.

The Home Run King never sits with his back to the door of a restaurant. He doesn't know who might walk in and surprise him. "When I'm driving and I see someone coming up in the rearview mirror," he says, "I watch him very carefully." He never lets down his guard in a room full of strangers. *Study everyone in a group without revealing yourself. What does he want? What's she going to do?* So often, he says with satisfaction, he guesses right.

Just some old habits from the Chase, he repeats. Habits he acquired in the summer of '73, the summer of Nixon and Dean and Sirica, of Aaron and Ruth, the summer that changed America and Hank Aaron forever.

Above all, says the major leagues' alltime home run, RBI, extra-base hit and total-bases leader, he observes this rule: Avoid ballparks. Fans pester him for autographs; dress him down in foul language if he declines; want to talk, talk, talk baseball with the King, when all he wants is to be left alone. He must be careful.

"Even now, assassination is always in the back of his mind," says Atlanta police major Calvin Wardlaw, his friend now and his bodyguard then, the man who carried the loaded .38 that long-ago summer when Aaron chased Babe Ruth's ghost. "There's always that possibility someone will try to make a name at this late date."

IT IS EARLY October, the afternoon of Game 1 of the National League Championship Series. In a few hours 51,971 people will file past the statue on the southeast side of Atlanta–Fulton County Stadium: a 15-foot-high bronze Aaron in full swing, mounted on a seven-foot-high block of white marble. The bronze engravings on the base make a powerful case that here played the greatest hitter who ever lived.

Before the game begins, an 84-year-old man will stand proudly in front of that statue wearing his battered old porkpie hat, a thick blue sweater vest and a skinny black-and-white striped tie. He'll stand for picture after picture, smiling in this one, shedding tears in that one, because the statue is of his son. "You know it's a big occasion," Hank Aaron likes to say, "if Daddy wears a tie."

Hank's wife, Billye, a former Atlanta TV talk-show host, will attend the game with his sister Gloria, the two of them dressed for the social outing of the year. They'll mingle with Ted Turner and Jane Fonda, Georgia governor Zell Miller and former Atlanta mayor Andrew Young. Hank's other sister, Alfredia, will be there too, and his daughter Gaile, son Hank Jr. and daughter Dorinda will use some of the dozen or more tickets their father has bought for friends and family.

Dorinda is 30, but her father still calls her "the baby." Earlier in the week she was chagrined by the figure she saw on a Wheaties box in the grocery store: Willie Mays again! "They never remember Daddy," she explains now. "Daddy has to be there tonight." But he will not be at the game tonight. Instead, the King will stay behind his wall, a prisoner of memory.

As Aaron sits in his living room while his family prepares to leave for the stadium without him, his habitually stoic expression softens. His large brown eyes—they are his mother's eyes, everyone says—well up the way a man's do when his will resists his deepest emotions. The tears are coming hard now, fastballs on the fists, and Hank Aaron is just getting around in time, barely getting a piece, hanging in.

"It should have been the happiest time of my life, the best year," he says of 1973. "But it was the worst year. It was hell. So many bad things happened. . . . Things I'm still trying to get over, and maybe never will. Things I know I'll never forget.

"I don't want to forget."

WHAT DOES IT SAY of America that a man fulfills the purest of American dreams, struggling up from Jim Crow poverty to dethrone the greatest of Yankee kings . . . yet feels not like a hero but like someone hunted, haunted?

What does it say of baseball that the man who hit more doubles, triples and home runs than anyone else can't sit back and enjoy it?

What does it say of the man?

"He is very wary of people because he's been burned," says Lonnie Wheeler, coauthor of *I Had a Hammer: The Hank Aaron Story.* "You see that in all his dealings—social contacts, business contacts. He proceeds very deliberately. It's partly a personality thing. He's very inward. And I think the Ruth chase still affects him. You don't go through that without scars, and he still has them."

It has been 18 years since Hank Aaron hit Nos. 714 and 715 and kept on hammering to an epic 755; 16 years since he retired; 10 years since he was inducted into the Hall of Fame. The Home Run King is a grandfather now, and by tradition he should be lionized, a legend in the autumn of his life. But Henry Aaron takes no comfort in baseball immortality, in lore and remembrance. He says, "I never think about those things."

Watching the Braves and Pirates on TV, the Gants and Bondses flickering across the screen, he never thinks, *It used to be Aaron and Clemente.* As the CBS cameras capture the left-field placard that reads HANK AARON NO. 715, sentiment does not stir in Aaron. The King never discusses the home run that moved him ahead of Ruth. "It brings back too many unpleasant memories," he says. That, he tells you, was another life.

The symbols of that life, the artifacts of glory, mean little to him. You'll look in vain in Aaron's house for his 500th home run ball; for the 536th, which tied Mickey Mantle; for the 600th, the 700th, the 714th; for his 3,000th hit; for the 1957 National League MVP Award or the '56 and '59 league batting-champ trophies. Go to Cooperstown or to the house of Aaron's parents in Mobile, if you want to see all that. The 755th home run bat and ball, the crown jewels of the Home Run King? Tucked away in the vault of an Atlanta bank. All of it banished for lack of significance.

In the kitchen is something he kept: a newspaper story, posted on a cabinet. The headline reads HALL OF FAME THROWS AARON A CURVE. The writer decries the terrible injustice that nine voters somehow thought Aaron wasn't worthy of Cooperstown, keeping the Home Run King from entering by unanimous vote. The story is 10 years old. This is the sort of thing Hank Aaron keeps.

His father is entering the kitchen now, a stooped old man walking slowly, picking his way through the mists of memory. Herbert Aaron raises his head to look at his son and says softly, "Who was that boy that caught that home run?"

"I don't know what you're talking about," Hank says.

It's a familiar dance, the father struggling to remember, the son gently nudging him toward his goal. Of all his son's home runs, Herbert cherishes one the most. He imagines the Braves in Milwaukee again, his son 23 again, the autumn of '57 again, two outs in the 11th inning and Henry Aaron hitting the home run that beats the St. Louis Cardinals, the one that earns "Bushville's Braves" their first pennant and makes Eddie Mathews and Warren Spahn and all those white Braves carry skinny, black number 44 off the field in jubilation. Henry was the league MVP that season, already a star, but that home run convinced his father of something more important, that his son had no fear.

The moment is proudly displayed in Herbert's den in Mobile, captured in a tiny framed dispatch from the Youngstown (Ohio) *Vindicator* of Sept. 24, 1957, under the headline NEGRO MOBBED IN MILWAUKEE. On the same day that police tried to protect black schoolchildren from white mobs in Little Rock, the story says, white mobs chased a Negro in Beer City to "make him mayor of Milwaukee."

Now the old man says, "I mean, who's that boy who caught that home run when you won the pennant in Milwaukee?"

"That boy was named Muffett," Hank says gently. "Billy Muffett. I don't know who caught the ball, Daddy. Muffett was the one who pitched it." Herbert's face radiates pride all over again. So much sweeter was that homer, No. 109, than any that came 16 years later, in that awful summer when Herbert's wife prayed and wept over the agony of her third son.

Now Hank says, "I've got to go and get you some clothes." His father has driven up from Mobile without packing enough. So Hank climbs up to the attic and digs out some clothes and comes upon something else, a simple cardboard box. A box of letters 20 years old. This, above all things, Hank wanted to keep. "This," he says, "changed me."

He averts his eyes. This is nothing to confront now, not on a lovely fall day with his father in town. He opens this box only when something happens to stir the hurt deep in his heart. Then the only thing that seems real, the only thing that redeems him, is to sit and read his fan mail again. On such days he opens the box in his attic and looses all the evils of his world.

Dear Hank Aaron,

Retire or die! . . . You'll be in Shea Stadium July 6-8, and in Philly July 9th to 11th. . . . You will die in one of those games. I'll shoot you in one of them.

Dirty old nigger man,

Had Ruth played and been at bat as many times as you, old nigger, he would have hit. . . 1100 home runs. . . . I hope lightning strikes you old man four-flusher.

Dear Hank Aaron,

How about some sickle cell anemia, Hank?

Do you remember how we made epic heroes of other men? Joe DiMaggio, divine grace in human form. . . Sweet-swinging Ted Williams, Poseidon to DiMaggio's Apollo. . . Mickey Mantle, Achilles. . . O mighty Zeus, Babe Ruth.

Hank Aaron remembers.

And what do you remember about Hank Aaron?

Awfully quiet, wasn't he? Quick wrists, otherwise deliberate, slow. A quiet man who played in quiet towns.

Do you remember the stereotypes that sportswriters applied to Aaron in the '50s, descriptions of the country Negro who didn't talk or think much, jus' swung the stick, took his time shufflin' that "Satchel posterior" around the bases?

Hank Aaron remembers.

Babe Ruth's myth is so great that he has entered the American vernacular (Ruthian: larger than life). Yet baseball's living, reigning Home Run King is uncelebrated, his story seldom told: his rise from Alabama poverty, his quiet, heroic battles against racism in baseball, his proud carrying of the torch passed down by Jackie Robinson. Where were his mythmakers?

Aaron says he would settle for being remembered as hardworking, humble, shy—and as the owner of so many of the game's significant hitting records. But those same qualities that made Joe DiMaggio a hero made Aaron an enigma.

Aaron is sitting in his office at the CNN Center, staring out at the purple hills of northern Georgia. He has shut his office door, asked his secretary to hold his calls. Earlier this year, for the first time in 39 years Aaron stopped making his living exclusively at the ballpark. He got a promotion, he says proudly. He is now a vice president of Turner Broadcasting. His job is to get CNN monitors in every airport in America. With his other business interests and the work he still does for the Braves, he makes at least twice the $250,000 he made in his best earning year as a ballplayer.

The man behind the desk, the man in the expensive gray suit and gold-rimmed spectacles, is fighting back tears. "I think about things that happened," he says, and trails off.

"My brother has lots of good memories from baseball and lots of bad memories," says his sister Alfredia Aaron-Scott, "but the bad memories are more profound. If someone dumps urine on your head during a game, it can spoil everything, spoil the two home runs you hit that day. Henry was always so quiet. But now he's talking more than he ever has. I think my brother wants people to know what he suffered."

THE HOUSE IN Mobile where Henry Aaron grew up now has plumbing, electricity and windows. The pigs are gone and the outhouse is gone and Daddy's moonshine stash is gone and the dirt ditch out front is filled and paved. But Mama's still there, sitting on the porch in southern Alabama, catching some sun. Her husband is puttering around the house in his porkpie hat, waiting for her to fry up the trout she caught in the Mobile River.

The woman, in her late 70's now, her eyes hard, says, "Henry had everything that could happen to a black boy happen to him, and it hurt him." She imagines, still, the train that took him away to the Negro leagues at 18, the two dollars and two sandwiches he carried. "You know if that's all his mama had to give him, he'd seen some hard times," she says. He was skinny as a toothpick, batted cross-handed because no one had told him not to, feared white pitchers because he'd heard they were a superior race.

Still, he dreamed of going on to the big leagues. Mama told him, "Gotta play a lot better than the white boy."

Daddy didn't tell him anything. "What was I gonna say?" Herbert asks.

Soon after he moved up from the Negro leagues to the farm system of the Milwaukee Braves, Henry Aaron went into Waycross, Ga., to get a haircut and missed the bus back to the Braves' minor league camp outside of town. As he walked back, it grew dark. He took a shortcut through the woods, he recalls, "and when I came out, the camp guard spotted me, and all he saw was a strange Negro, and he started shooting." Somehow Aaron crawled into the barracks alive. A few days later he and two other black players, Horace Garner and Felix Mantilla, were put onto a bus to Florida to play for Class A Jacksonville and break the color line in the Deep South.

Baseball's racial history is fixed on a single name and place and time—Jackie Robinson, Brooklyn, 1947. But Robinson didn't break baseball's color line for all of the U.S., only for the northern states. By 1953 the major leagues reached no farther south than Cincinnati, St. Louis and Washington, D.C. Aaron, Garner and Mantilla were the first blacks ever to play for Jacksonville. And so began a season of epithets ("Hey, nigger, why you runnin'? There's no watermelon out there!") and death threats from fans and of racial taunts from opposing players and coaches.

Aaron took it stoically. Took Jacksonville to a pennant. Took home the MVP trophy. Now, from a distance of 40 years, Aaron says that what he heard in Jacksonville was "small-time stuff." The young man was headed for the big leagues.

The Milwaukee Braves' skipper, Charlie Grimm, called his rookie outfielder Stepin Fetchit because he "just keeps shuffling along." Warren Spahn was happy to have a player of Stepin Fetchit's skills on his side. "What's black and catches flies?" the Hall of Fame southpaw liked to joke. "The Braves' outfield."

In the '60s the National League All-Star team was dominated by black players. Aaron, Mays, Ernie Banks, Willie McCovey, Billy Williams and Willie Stargell met nearly every year at the midsummer classic and swapped stories—the kind of stories, Aaron says, that "made it clear that we could never forget we were black ballplayers."

Williams had been so angered by being forced to eat in restaurant kitchens in San Antonio that he quit his minor league team. In Plainview, Texas, a white man had put a gun to the head of Stargell and said, "Nigger, if you play in that game tonight, I'll blow your brains out." Aaron contributed Sally League horror stories.

"But I was only 19 in the Sally League," he says now. "It was like sending a 19-year-old into war. What did I know about death? What did I know about the world? It didn't matter so much then.

"Later, it mattered."

THE LETTERS CAME from every state, but most were postmarked in northern cities. They came in an avalanche, 3,000 a day. They were filled with hate. More hate than Aaron had ever imagined.

He got a plaque from the U.S. Postal Service for receiving more mail than anyone else in the U.S. except politicians— 930,000 pieces. Aaron's bodyguard, Wardlaw, tried to hide the most vile letters—like one with a picture of a gorilla that said, "This is your mother." Dick Cecil, then a Braves vice president, says he too tried to shield Aaron from missives that spewed hate but contained no assassination threats. The death threats, of course, were put into plastic bags and shipped right to the FBI.

Dear Hank,

You are a very good ballplayer, but if you come close to Babe Ruth's 714 homers I have a contract out on you. . . . If by the all star game you have come within 20 homers of Babe you will be shot on sight by one of my assassins on July 24, 1973.

Hey nigger boy,

We at the KKK Staten island Division want you to know that no number of guards can keep you dirty son of a bitch nigger—alive.

WHATEVER OTHER LETTERS Aaron could lay his hands on, the milder ones, he asked his secretary to save. And all that year, in public appearances off the field, he tried to put a smile on his careworn face. Why, there was Hank Aaron on *The Flip Wilson Show*! Wasn't that the Hammer cooking with Dinah Shore? Did you see Hank on *Hollywood Squares*?

Because of the threats, Aaron spent his free time sitting in his Atlanta apartment, watching a neon sign outside blink on and off. On the road Paul Casanova, a catcher for the Braves, brought meals to Aaron's room. Aaron didn't stay with the team, didn't eat with the team, just as in Jim Crow days. Every off day Aaron, by then divorced from his wife, Barbara, flew to Nashville to visit their daughter Gaile at Fisk University. The FBI had uncovered a plot to kidnap Gaile; she finished the term protected by federal agents disguised as maintenance men.

During home stands Aaron was bitter about the Braves' paltry attendance: The 1,362 fans, then a record low, who watched him hit No. 711 seemed to reflect the apathy, if not disdain, that Atlanta felt for him. The Braves' front office received threats on Aaron's life, and one time the team had to deny a rumor that he had been shot. Another time, during a game in Montreal, a firecracker exploded, and Aaron, standing in leftfield, thought it was all over. "It scared me out of my mind," he says now.

Aaron displayed "greater courage and dignity than any man I've ever seen," says Cecil. He also hit .301 with 40 homers in only 392 at bats, as fine a season as a 39-year-old ever had. He finished with 713 home runs, one short of Ruth.

Hi Hank!

There is 6 months until the '74 season begins. Until then, one can break a leg, his back, develop sickle cell anemia or drop dead. Babe Ruth's 714 record will never be tied or broken.

Dear Hank:

I hope lightning will strike you before next season.

In his first at bat of the '74 season, facing Jack Billingham in Cincinnati, Aaron hit No. 714, tying the Babe, and his eyes welled up as he rounded third base. That night Hank called his mother in Mobile and said, "I'm going to save the next one for you, Mom."

Estella Aaron remembers, "He told me, 'Mama, let them try to kill me. That makes me more determined than ever to set that record.' " The FBI was investigating threats that if Aaron hit No. 715, he would not cross home plate alive.

On April 8, 1974, Herbert Aaron, one of 53,775 fans in Atlanta–Fulton County Stadium, the biggest crowd in Braves history, threw out the first ball. Next to Herb sat Alfredia and Estella. Henry's mom had put on her best diamond-print dress and had her hair coiffed for the occasion.

Al Downing was on the mound for the Dodgers. In the fourth inning, with the Braves losing 3–1 and Darrell Evans on first, Aaron swung at a Downing fastball, and baseball had a new Home Run King. There was chaos on the field.

As her son rounded first base, the diminutive Estella "just flew over the railing," recalls Alfredia. "I was so scared. I said to my husband, 'Go get Mama!' "

As Aaron rounded second base, two college students appeared and ran alongside him. He pushed one of them away with his arm. In the stands Wardlaw touched his binoculars case with the gun inside and thought, Should I go out there? Should I stay? "It was the hardest decision of my life," he says now.

At the plate Mathews and Evans and all the Braves were waiting to mob the new Home Run King . . . but a woman in her early 60s, her cap of hair stiff in the breeze as she ran, got to him first.

"Mama just jumped into Henry's arms and squeezed him around the neck and put a hammerlock on him," Alfredia says. "They couldn't get her off him. She just wouldn't let go. Later, I said, 'Mama, what in Lord's name were you doing?' She wasn't running out there out of happiness. She was running out there because she thought her son was going to die. She told me, 'If they were going to kill my son, they were going to have to kill me, too.' "

THE MORNING AFTER Game 1 of the 1992 NLCS, Hank Aaron shuts his office door at the CNN Center, removes his gold-rimmed spectacles and says, "Hank Aaron, Willie Mays, Willie McCovey, Roberto Clemente, Ernie Banks, Lou Brock, Frank Robinson, Bob Gibson—we came along and saved what would have become the dullest game in history. We brought excitement, speed. We paid our dues, man. No one knows what we had to go through—get off the bus, go get dressed somewhere else, go eat on the other side of town, get back in half an hour ready to play. What has baseball done for us? How many of those guys are around the game today? The white man allowed us a few crumbs. 'You can sit right here in the front of the bus so long as you're pulling in money. After that, it's back to the back of the bus.' "

The vice president's smooth corporate monotone is gone; his voice is growing loud, harsh. "They say we don't have the 'mental necessities' to sit behind the desk, we just have God-given talent. But, man, I had to work hard too. I had to think. I didn't have any more natural talent than Ted Williams or Joe DiMaggio. I played the game 23 years, and that tells me I had to study some pitchers pretty well. But no—I was a 'dumb s.o.b.' It's racism. These things really anger me."

The latest things to anger Aaron are racial slurs attributed to Cincinnati Reds' owner Marge Schott. Two weeks ago, it was reported that in a December 1991 deposition Schott gave in response to a lawsuit by a former employee, she acknowledged having used the word nigger in conversation and said it was "possible" that she had referred to the birthday of Martin Luther King Jr. as "Nigger Day." She denied reports that she had referred to former Reds players Eric Davis and Dave Parker as her "million-dollar niggers."

Aaron spoke out immediately, telling *The Cincinnati Enquirer*, "Baseball must come forward and make it known to the world: We won't stand for this. There is no place for it in the national pastime.... Baseball must investigate."

In his office now, Aaron's hands are chopping the air. "People say I'm bitter, but they haven't walked a mile in my shoes. Arthur Ashe said it was harder for him to be a black person in this country than to have AIDS, and I can understand it. You're on trial every day. I go into a department store and they wait on the white man first, even if this black man's been waiting 20 minutes longer. Happens every day. If I wasn't Hank Aaron, who hit 755 home runs, I'd be just another nigger.

"People say, 'I can't see how your cards sell for so much less than Mickey Mantle's,' like $2,000 for my top card to

$25,000 for his. He had a great career; I had a great career too. It's racism.

"Funny how Babe Ruth's 714 home runs was the most impressive, unbreakable record in sports until a black man broke it. Then it shifted. Now it's DiMaggio's hitting streak."

On the walls of Aaron's office are pictures of him with presidents Ford and Carter, with Henry Kissinger and Ted Turner. There are honorary degrees. There is little to suggest that this is the office of the greatest home run hitter who ever lived.

But this thought sustains him. A century from now someone will open *The Baseball Encyclopedia* and go no further than the first name: Aaron, Henry Louis, a shade behind Pete Rose and Ty Cobb with 3,771 hits, and the alltime leader in home runs (755), RBIs (2,297), extra-base hits (1,477) and total bases (6,856—a full 722 ahead of the next guy, Stan Musial).

By then Aaron will at last be at peace, under a simple headstone: "Just 'Here lies Hank Aaron, born 1934, died whenever,' " he says. "No use paying a long tribute. They didn't do it when I was playing, no use doing it when I'm dead."

THE OLD WOMAN walks slowly from the frying pan, sets down a platter of trout fillets, a bowl of corn, a hunk of bread, and says, "Sit right here. That's where he sat as a boy."

She raps a deeply lined knuckle on the table. She says, "Tell him he's got to forget, got to let go. He can't worry about things you can't control. He's got to put his faith in the Lord. God wanted him to have that record. He didn't steal it. He earned it. I tell him no one can take it away from him nohow.

On most days he is warmed by friends and a large and adoring family, warmed by a wife who urges him to see all the love in the world. He has opportunities to open his heart to others as few men can. Aaron spends long hours each year reaching out to the children of Big Brothers/Big Sisters, for which he has raised more than $7 million. He met a woman in the street, a mother from the projects who didn't have food for her babies, and it made him think of another mother, long ago, who often didn't have food for her babies. He sent his secretary to take the woman to the supermarket to buy her enough food to last a long time. He wants children to know that even if they're poor and black, they can still achieve a dream.

Earlier this year he spent a weekend signing autographs at a card show in Miami, for which he was paid about $25,000. He met up with Paul Casanova, the player who brought him his meals during the Chase. The old catcher had fallen on some hard times. When Aaron left Miami, he left the $25,000 with Casanova.

The letters still come in bagfuls to the CNN Center in Atlanta, to the offices of the Braves, to the Hall of Fame in Cooperstown. They begin, "Dear Hank Aaron" or "Dear Home Run King." The King is only human, so he reads them.

Dear Hank Aaron:

Thanks for all the great years you had with the Braves. You were my Dad's favorite player.

Dear Hank Aaron:

I play little league, and you are my most favorite baseball player.

WHILE AARON is cynical about autograph hounds—"Collectors just out to make money," he says—the children who write to him touch him deeply, and he signs his name for them all.

Recently the grandmother of an Alabama boy wrote asking Aaron to call the child. He was dying of leukemia. Aaron phoned him in the hospital, but the boy was in isolation for bone-marrow treatments. The boy later died, and Aaron sent a $1,500 check to his family to help cover expenses.

But Aaron still receives other kinds of letters, too:

Mr. Henry (Hank) Aaron,

You are bitter and upset because you were not the first nigger manager. All you black bastards do is complain and demand. Now I know why they lynched you people in the south.

Mr. Hank Aaron,

. . . I think Mr. Aaron in all fairness you should make a statement . . . that you had more at bats than Babe Ruth, after all Babe Ruth was a super great baseball player and is a credit to the white race.

THESE ARE THE LETTERS he remembers most, the ones he reads after he has been subjected to behavior that is rude or racist. At a ball game seven or eight years ago, Aaron says, a woman asked him for his autograph. "I'm sorry, ma'am," he said. "I'm busy watching one of my pitchers. When I'm all done, I'll be happy to give you an autograph." When Aaron went over to the woman's box and offered his signature, she coldly declined it.

Later that day Aaron climbed again into his attic. Not to read the letters from fans who had named their high schools and their children after him, the folks who wrote saying that home run No. 715 was more important than the moonshot. Not to read one of the 20,000 congratulatory telegrams he received on April 9, 1974.

As he still does on such days, Aaron read other letters, letters of hatred and cruelty and ignorance that America once sent its Home Run King, missives that break his heart but somehow sustain him. When he broke Babe Ruth's record, Aaron says, "my real job was only starting." He says he saw that God must have chosen him to break the record for a reason—not just to clear fences but to hammer down walls. He promised to use the record "like a Louisville Slugger." He vowed, 18 years ago, never to forget.

In the vast stillness of his wooded estate, in the long quiet of his reign, the Home Run King keeps taking his cuts. Pain and redemption are joined now, like bat to ball. "I read the letters," he says, "because they remind me not to be surprised or hurt.

"They remind me what people are really like."

◇

One for the Ages

BY RON FIMRITE

*SI named Hank Aaron, then 60, one of the most influential
sports figures of the previous 40 years. Here's why*

HE SEEMED ALWAYS TO BE THE LONELIEST OF MEN, AND
never more so than on the occasion of his greatest triumph.
Henry Aaron had been such an unpretentious and workman-
like star that he caught the baseball world by surprise when it
became obvious in the early 1970s that he would soon surpass
Babe Ruth as the game's most prolific home run hitter. By the
end of the '73 season, in fact, he was only one homer shy of the
Babe's career record of 714. Now—at last, and yet suddenly—
Hank Aaron stood poised on the brink of immortality.

The brink seemed to Aaron more like a frightening precipice.
He had never received a particle of the adulation lavished on
such contemporaries as Willie Mays, Mickey Mantle and
Roberto Clemente. The others had a glamour sorely missing in
Aaron's placid makeup. Hank did his job every day, and that's
exactly the way he wanted it. Now he found himself standing in
the white-hot glare of the media spotlight. He was about to beat

the Babe, for god's sake! But Aaron embraced one aspect of his record chase: As a black man from Mobile and as one of the pioneers who helped break down the game's color barrier in the '50s, he felt a surge of racial pride at the history-making element of his impending accomplishment. In his years in Atlanta he had sharpened an already keen social conscience. Beating the Babe, he knew, would be a statement.

But Aaron didn't much care for the rest of this home run circus—the invasion of his cherished privacy, the daily interruptions of his work schedule, the inevitable harassment of his family and friends. And there was something else, something he didn't fully acknowledge in public until years later. As he approached the record, Aaron became the target of a virulent hate-mail campaign. By what right, the racists wanted to know, did he, a black man, dare to supplant the beloved Babe?

But Aaron beat the Babe anyway. In his first swing of the bat in the 1974 season, he homered off the Reds' Jack Billingham in Cincinnati to tie the record. And then, four days later, on a rainy Monday night in Atlanta, he lifted a fastball thrown by the Los Angeles Dodgers' Al Downing over the leftfield fence for number 715. Aaron circled the bases in the unwanted company of two young fans who had rushed onto the field to applaud him. Aaron eyed them warily. At home plate Hank was joined by his father, Herbert, and his mother, Estella. Georgia governor Jimmy Carter was also there to congratulate him. An American flag had been painted on the grass in centerfield. Bands were playing, the crowd was cheering. Hammerin' Hank had done it! Only to him did it seem a hollow victory.

Aaron would complete his 23-year career where he started it, in Milwaukee. He played two more years there, with the Brewers, finishing with 755 home runs and a major league–record 2,297 runs batted in. He had led the National League in homers and runs batted in four times, won two batting championships and, in 1957, been the league's Most Valuable Player; but he didn't receive the recognition that was his due until the very end, when it could scarcely be savored.

In his 1991 book, *I Had a Hammer*, Aaron unleashed much of the anger and disappointment he had harbored for nearly 20 years. It is a sad irony that his status as an American hero has been elevated by the revelation of the indignities he endured. Meanwhile Aaron, at 60, presses on. As a Braves executive since his retirement from competition, in 1976, he has campaigned tirelessly to persuade the baseball powers to hire more African-Americans in front-office positions. In his still quietly efficient way, Aaron seems to be his own best argument.

◇

POSTSCRIPT: *Aaron would remain a keen social conscience for the game, continuing to push for more black executives in the majors. Major League Baseball, in turn, reached out to the Home Run King, announcing in 1999 (the 25th anniversary of Number 715) the creation of the Hank Aaron Award to be given each year to the league's top hitter. Three years later, President George W. Bush presented Aaron with the Presidential Medal of Freedom, the nation's highest civilian honor.*

◇

Acknowledgments

IF YOU ARE YOUNGER than 35, chances are, you never saw
Henry Aaron wield his mighty hammer. Consequently, perhaps
more than any other collection that SPORTS ILLUSTRATED has put
together, this anthology has leaned on the magazine's earliest generations of writers. SI owes a special debt to Roy Terrell, Jack
Mann, William Leggett, Ron Fimrite, Larry Keith and the inim-
itable George Plimpton, who between them spent more than 12
decades at the magazine, as well as Dick Young and Mike Capuzzo,
both of whom left their own indelible marks as non-SI staffers.
Still, this book would not have been possible without the collective
sweat and muscle of numerous current SI staffers, who somehow
found time, while putting out a weekly magazine, to work on this
project: Rob Fleder, Kevin Kerr, Steve Hoffman, Steven Charny,
Caitlin Moscatello, Ed Truscio, Craig Gartner, Nate Gordon, Greg
Kelly, Stefanie Kaufman, Josh Denkin, Linda Verigan, Peggy Terry,
Jen Grad and, of course, SI's Managing Editor, Terry McDonell, for
whom the idea of *The Hammer* originally resonated.